**AMERICAN NURSES
ASSOCIATION**

HPNA
Hospice and Palliative
Nurses Association

ADVANCING EXPERT CARE IN SERIOUS ILLNESS

Scope AND
Standards
OF PRACTICE

Palliative Nursing

AN ESSENTIAL RESOURCE FOR HOSPICE AND PALLIATIVE NURSES

nurses THE PUBLISHING
books.org PROGRAM OF ANA

American Nurses Association
Silver Spring, Maryland
2014

American Nurses Association
8515 Georgia Avenue, Suite 400
Silver Spring, MD 20910-3492
1-800-274-4ANA
http://www.Nursingworld.org

Published by Nursesbooks.org
The Publishing Program of ANA
http://www.Nursesbooks.org/

The Hospice and Palliative Nurses Association (HPNA) is the professional organization that represents Palliative Nursing. Our members include hospice and palliative nurses and other members of the team. HPNA's mission is *to advance expert care in serious illness* through a focus on advancing expert communication skills, pain and symptom management, and coordination and transitions of care. HPNA seeks to support and engage members through our four pillars of education, advocacy, leadership, and research to achieve our vision of transforming the care and culture of serious illness.

The American Nurses Association is the only full-service professional organization representing the interests of the nation's 3.1 million registered nurses through its constituent/state nurses associations and its organizational affiliates. The ANA advances the nursing profession by fostering high standards of nursing practice, promoting the rights of nurses in the workplace, projecting a positive and realistic view of nursing, and by lobbying the Congress and regulatory agencies on healthcare issues affecting nurses and the public.

ISBN-13: 978-1-55810-539-3   SAN: 851-3481   02/2015R

First printing: January 2014.
Second printing: November 2014. Third printing: February 2015.

Contents

Contributors

Editors

Constance M. Dahlin, APRN-BC, ACHPN®, FPCN, FAAN

Dena Jean Sutermaster, RN, MSN, CHPN®

Reviewers

Joan "Jody" Chrastek, DNP, RN, CHPN®

Barbara Daly, PhD, RN, FAAN

Jennifer Gentry, ANP, ACHPN®, FPCN

Nancy L. Grandovic, RN, BSN, MEd, CHPN®

Barbara Head, PhD, RN, CHPN®, ACSW, FPCN

Judy Lentz, RN, MSN, NHA

JoAnne Reifsnyder, PhD, RN

Caroline Schauer, RN, MSN, CHPN®

Deanna Tansey RN, BSN, CHPN®

Sally Welsh, MSN, RN, NEA-BC

Christine Westphal, NP, MSN, ACNS-BC, ACHPN®, CCRN

ANA Staff

Carol J. Bickford, PhD, RN-BC, CPHIMS – Content editor

Maureen E. Cones, Esq. – Legal counsel

Yvonne Daley Humes – Project coordinator

Eric Wurzbacher, BA – Project editor

About the Hospice and Palliative Nurses Association

The Hospice and Palliative Nurses Association (HPNA) is the professional organization that represents Palliative Nursing. Our members include hospice and palliative nurses and other members of the team. HPNA's mission is *to advance expert care in serious illness* through a focus on advancing expert communication skills, pain and symptom management, and coordination and transitions of care. HPNA seeks to support and engage members through our four pillars of education, advocacy, leadership, and research to achieve our vision of transforming the care and culture of serious illness.

About the American Nurses Association

The American Nurses Association (ANA) is the only full-service professional organization representing the interests of the nation's 3.1 million registered nurses through its constituent/state nurses associations and its organizational affiliates. The ANA advances the nursing profession by fostering high standards of nursing practice, promoting the rights of nurses in the workplace, projecting a positive and realistic view of nursing, and by lobbying the Congress and regulatory agencies on health care issues affecting nurses and the public.

About Nursesbooks.org,
The Publishing Program of ANA

Nursesbooks.org publishes books on ANA core issues and programs, including ethics, leadership, quality, specialty practice, advanced practice, and the profession's enduring legacy. Best known for the foundational documents of the profession on nursing ethics, scope and standards of practice, and social policy, Nursesbooks.org is the publisher for the professional, career-oriented nurse, reaching and serving nurse educators, administrators, managers, and researchers as well as staff nurses in the course of their professional development.

Preface

Palliative care nursing reflects a "whole-person" philosophy of care implemented across the lifespan and across diverse health care settings. The patient and family is the unit of care. The goal of palliative nursing is to promote quality of life along the illness trajectory through the relief of suffering, and this includes care of the dying and bereavement follow-up for the family and significant others in the patient's life.
(Coyle, 2010, p. 5)

The mission of the Hospice and Palliative Nurses Association (HPNA) is to "Advance expert care in serious illnesses." This is accomplished through four pillars of excellence that guide the work of the organization: education, advocacy, leadership, and research. The pillar of education is represented by HPNA as the primary resource and voice for state-of-the-art palliative nursing knowledge. The pillar of advocacy is represented by HPNA as the leading voice for patients, families, and nurses in the transformation of the care and culture of serious or life-threatening illness. The pillar of leadership is represented by HPNA as an organization empowering its nurse members to transform the care and culture of serious or life-threatening illness. The pillar of research is represented by HPNA as it translates evidence about the care and culture of serious or life-threatening illness into action. In accordance with its mission statement, HPNA revises its Scope and Standards of Practice to reflect the current principles and practice of palliative nursing in the changing healthcare landscape. The current edition, *Palliative Nursing: Scope and Standards of Practice—An Essential Resource for Hospice and Palliative Nurses* has evolved from a limited perspective on hospice nursing to a full text reflecting the expanded perspectives of palliative nursing, which encompasses both hospice and palliative nurses.

Definition of Palliative Care

The Hospice and Palliative Nurses Association endorses the exact definition of *palliative care* originating from the National Consensus Project for Quality Palliative Care (NCP), which states: "*Palliative Care* means patient and family-centered care that optimizes quality of life by anticipating, preventing, and treating suffering. Palliative care throughout the continuum of illness involves addressing the physical, intellectual, emotional, social, and spiritual needs and [facilitating] patient autonomy, access to information, and choice" (NCP, 2013, p. 9). The National Consensus Project further explains, "Palliative care is operationalized through effective management of pain and other distressing symptoms, while incorporating psychosocial and spiritual care with consideration of patient/family needs, preferences, values, beliefs, and culture. Evaluation and treatment should be comprehensive and patient-centered with a focus on the central role of the family unit in decision-making. Palliative care affirms life by supporting the patient and family's goals for the future, including their hopes for cure or life-prolongation, as well as their hopes for peace and dignity throughout the course of illness, the dying process, and death" (NCP, 2013, p. 9).

The realm of palliative care services is individualized to the patient and family, occurring in the context of the diagnosis and time of initiation of services. Palliative care includes supportive counseling services, pain and symptom management, discharge planning, hospice care, and bereavement services after death. Palliative care may be delivered simultaneously with life-prolonging therapies, during all phases of illness. However, there are specific assumptions that underlie palliative care (NCP, 2013):

- Palliative care is patient- and family-centered care across the spectrum of illness.

- Palliative care begins with supportive care at the time of diagnosis of a serious or life-threatening illness and ends with bereavement care after death. Patient and family goals are supported throughout the course of illness, during the dying process, and after death, with respect to values, preferences, and beliefs. Palliative nursing is developmentally, culturally, ethnically, and spiritually appropriate.

- Palliative care relieves physical, psychological, emotional, and spiritual suffering of patients and families with serious or life-threatening illness.

- Palliative care is equitable, comprehensive, and reaches across health settings, with an emphasis on continuity, quality, safety, and access with attention to vulnerable populations and transitions of care. Services are available concurrently with or independent of curative or life-prolonging care.

- Palliative care is interdisciplinary and collaborative. Palliative care team members have clinical expertise and communication skills to educate patients about their disease, treatment options, and decision-making while maintaining confidentiality.

Palliative care expanded from the hospice model, which was initially based on the care of cancer patients. Due to the predictable cancer illness trajectory, the role of palliative care clearly increases as the cancer progresses. However, when palliative care is delivered to patients with noncancer diagnoses, the trajectory is less predictable. There are often periods of stabilization and exacerbations, resulting in more variable palliative care needs. Instead of a linear progression, there is a stepwise or wave progression of care (see Figure 1). As a patient's

FIGURE 1. Trajectories of Palliative Care

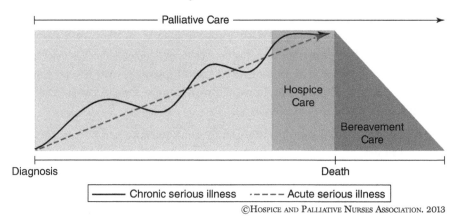

©HOSPICE AND PALLIATIVE NURSES ASSOCIATION. 2013

prognosis shortens to the last six months of life, hospice care may be initiated per patient and family preference. Palliative care continues through this time into bereavement. Support after the patient's death consists of acknowledging common psychological and physical symptoms as the result of grief and loss, and counseling on coping with loss, as well as providing information about the completion of necessary financial and legal tasks.

Several studies have demonstrated the improvement of quality of life and survival in patients who received early palliative care at diagnosis (Bakitas et al., 2009; Temel et al., 2010). Further research has focused on which illnesses are best suited to palliative care. During the 2011 National Institute of Nursing Research (NINR) conference, "The Science of Compassion: Future Directions in End-of-Life and Palliative Care," palliative care research was highlighted for its continued commitment to "comprehensive, bio-behavioral research to improve health and health outcomes, including the quality of care provided at the end of life (EOL)" (National Institute of Nursing Research [NINR], 2011, p. 3). The Hospice and Palliative Nurses Association's *2012–2015 Research Agenda* prioritized the structure and process of care, physical aspects of care, and psychological and psychiatric aspects of care as domains needing further study (Hospice and Palliative Nurses Association [HPNA], 2011a).

Scope of Palliative Nursing Practice

Definition and Description

Palliative nursing embraces and reflects a holistic philosophy of care provided to patients with serious or life-threatening illness in diverse health settings, across the lifespan. Palliative nursing is an evidence-based nursing practice that includes "the assessment, diagnosis, and treatment of human responses to actual or potential life-limiting illnesses within the context of a dynamic caring relationship with the patient and family, in order to reduce or relieve suffering and optimize health" (Lynch, Dahlin, Hultman, & Coakley, 2011). *Health* is defined as the "wholeness, integrity, quality of life, and function of the person" (Lynch, Dahlin, Hultman, & Coakley, 2011).

Palliative nursing focuses on care delivery to individual patients and families, patients within specific disease populations, and palliative care issues within health care and society as a whole entity. Inherent in palliative nursing are the processes of evaluation, treatment, and management within the eight domains of palliative care outlined in the National Consensus Project: Domain 1. Structure and Processes of Care; Domain 2. Physical Aspects of Care; Domain 3. Psychological and Psychiatric Aspects of Care; Domain 4. Social Aspects of Care; Domain 5. Spiritual, Religious, and Existential Aspects of Care; Domain 6. Cultural Aspects of Care; Domain 7. Care of the Patient at the End of Life; and Domain 8. Ethical and Legal Aspects of Care. This is accomplished through evidence-based physical, emotional, psychosocial, and spiritual or existential care, to individuals and families experiencing serious or life-threatening illness, within the matrix of an interdisciplinary care team that includes the patient and family. By eliciting patients' values, goals, and preferences of care, and advocating for them throughout the illness trajectory

(Lynch, Dahlin, Hultman, & Coakley, 2011), hospice and palliative nurses lead the comprehensive interdisciplinary collaborative care of the patient.

The essence of palliative nursing is honoring the individual patient in her or his journey; attending to psychological responses to the end of life, social and cultural factors, and spiritual aspects of care (NCP, 2013). From diagnosis to death, hospice and palliative nurses accompany the patient and her or his family with a goal of relieving suffering and promoting quality of life. The palliative nursing process includes holistic assessment of the patient and family, the offer or provision of information to allow more informed decision-making, meticulous pain and symptom management, determination and optimization of functional status, and support of coping patterns. "The [hospice and palliative] nurse's individual relationship with the patient and family is seen as a crucial [component of the care provided]. This relationship, together with knowledge and skills [to promote quality of life], is the essence of palliative care nursing and sets it apart from other areas of nursing practice" (Coyle, 2010, p. 5).

Across the spectrum of health settings, palliative nursing is expanding to respond to the dynamic nature of health care. Whereas historically only individuals with acute, serious, and life-threatening illnesses (e.g., severe trauma, acute stroke, and leukemia) with poor prognoses and poor quality of life received palliative care, palliative care has moved beyond the last months of life. Now, *serious or life-threatening illness* encompasses populations of patients of all ages within a broad and more expansive range of diagnostic categories, who are living with a persistent or recurring medical condition that adversely affects their daily functioning or will predictably reduce life expectancy (NCP, 2013, p. 8). Therefore, appropriate patients include those with serious diagnoses such as peripheral vascular disease, malignancies, renal or liver failure, devastating strokes, advanced heart or lung disease, frailty, neurodegenerative disorders, and the various forms of dementia; individuals living with chronic and life-threatening injuries from trauma; individuals with congenital injuries or conditions dependent on life-sustaining treatments and/or assistive care; and individuals with developmental and intellectual disabilities who develop serious or life-threatening illness (NCP, 2013).

Palliative nursing is provided for patients and families in a variety of locations, including inpatient, home, or residential hospice; acute care hospitals or palliative care units; long-term care facilities; rehabilitation facilities; home; ambulatory or outpatient palliative care primary care or specialty clinics; veterans' facilities; correctional facilities; homeless shelters; and mental health settings. Hospice and palliative nurses serve in a variety of roles including acting as expert clinicians, educators, researchers, administrators, consultants, case managers, program developers/coordinators, and/or policy-makers. Moreover, hospice and palliative nurses provide consistent responsibility for the round-the-clock care of palliative patients in these diverse settings. "Collaboration with other disciplines, within palliative care and in [the] broader context of the patient's care, is an essential skill for palliative nurses to obtain a more comprehensive view of the patient's issues and circumstance, explore options for care, and to advocate for patient's values, goals, and preferences" (Lynch, Dahlin, Hultman, & Coakley, 2011, p. 108). Hospice and palliative nurses work side-by-side with patients and families, physicians, social workers, chaplains, and other colleagues to determine each patient's unique goals, which are based on individual physical, psychosocial, emotional, and spiritual needs and factors.

A fundamental practice focus for palliative nursing is the management of clinical plans, not only for patients and families, but also for their interdisciplinary colleagues. The plan is established collaboratively between the patient and family (both as drivers of care) and the nurse in conjunction with the physician and other members of the interdisciplinary team. However, hospice and palliative nurses may work in roles in which they develop other education, policy initiatives, and quality plans on a local, regional, and national level. These plans include the assessment of community needs, ensuring high-quality palliative care in areas such as advance care planning, hospice and palliative services, pain and symptom management, and caring for patients with serious or life-threatening illness.

History and Evolution of Palliative Nursing

Palliative nursing evolved from hospice as the hospice philosophy moved into hospitals and academic settings. The concept of hospice antedates AD 475; the word itself derives from the Latin word *hospes,* meaning both host and guest. During the early Greek and Roman empires, self-sustained communities developed where ill, weary, homeless, and dying persons received care. This care of the whole person (i.e., soul, mind, and spirit) was provided throughout the Middle Ages by religious orders (e.g., monasteries, hospitaliers of the Crusades). In the 1800s, hospice evolved into care of the sick and incurables. As the term *hospice* became synonymous with care of the terminally ill, formal hospices were established: the Sisters of Charity founded Our Lady's Hospice in Dublin (1879) and St. Joseph's Hospice in London (1905). Concurrently, Florence Nightingale built the foundation of nursing, with its roots stemming from end-of-life caring for soldiers in the Crimean War (Berry, Volker, & Watson, 2010; Dahlin & Lynch, 2013).

Nurse leaders have been at the core of hospice development. Dame Cicely Saunders, a nurse, social worker, and physician, refined the concepts of modern hospice care in 1967 when she founded St. Christopher's Hospice in London, England. Dr. Florence Wald, Dean of the Yale School of Nursing, launched the American hospice movement through the development of a hospice nursing curriculum and the 1971 founding of the first hospice in the United States—Connecticut Hospice. The Tax Equity and Fiscal Responsibility Act of 1982 created the Medicare hospice benefit, which established formal recognition of hospice and its presence in United States health care (Berry, Volker, & Watson, 2010; Dahlin & Lynch, 2013). In 1987, the Hospice Nurses Association was formed to ensure quality hospice nursing that would allow hospice nursing to flourish.

In 1995, the first scope and standards for hospice nursing were developed. The landmark findings of SUPPORT (Study to Understand Prognoses and Preferences for Outcomes and Risks of Treatments) were published, highlighting high levels of pain experienced by seriously ill and dying patients, disrespect of patient preferences at end of life, and poor communication about end of life (SUPPORT Principal Investigators, 1995). Subsequently, the Robert Wood Johnson Foundation (RWJF) responded to the "overriding need to change the kind of care dying Americans receive" with financial support and commitment to end-of-life initiatives (Last Acts Task Force, 1997). This was followed by the Institute of Medicine report, *Approaching Death: Improving Care at End of Life,* which described the necessary changes for end-of-life care (Institute of Medicine [IOM], 1997).

Since then, significant nursing events have led to the establishment of the specialty of palliative nursing. Research revealed insufficient palliative care content in undergraduate nursing education. This led to the development of nursing practice competencies and nursing education on communication, ethics, and the principles of pain and symptom management (Ferrell, Virani, & Grant, 1999). The American Association of Colleges of Nursing (AACN), supported by RWJF, convened a round table of expert nurses to discuss and initiate educational change related to palliative care. These nurse experts developed the document *Peaceful Death,* which outlined baccalaureate competencies to be included in education (American Association of Colleges of Nursing [AACN], 1997). Other educational programs included the development of the End-of-Life Nursing Education Consortium (ELNEC)—a joint project between

AACN and the City of Hope National Medical Center. The number of nurses attending the variety of ELNEC offerings continues to increase significantly.

In 2001, nursing leaders from academia, clinical practice, and research held a national leadership meeting to discuss the vital role of advanced practice registered nurses in palliative care, and disseminated a white paper, entitled *Promoting Excellence in End-of-Life Care: A Position Statement from American Nursing Leaders* (Promoting Excellence in End-of-Life Care, 2002). HPNA published two position statements on the role of the nurse: *Value of the Professional Nurse in End-of-Life Care* (HPNA, 2004) and *Value of Advanced Practice Nurse in Palliative Care* (HPNA, 2007), which endorsed the Promoting Excellence in End-of-Life Care white paper and emphasized the importance of the role of nursing in palliative care. To reflect the practice of nurses with baccalaureate and graduate education as delineated in the Peaceful Death Competencies (AACN, 1997), HPNA produced the second edition of *Scope and Standards of Hospice and Palliative Nursing*.

In 2003, the American Nurses Association (ANA) formulated a position statement regarding the promotion of comfort and relief of pain of dying patients (ANA, 2003). This position statement was superseded by *Registered Nurses' Roles and Responsibilities in Providing Expert Care and Counseling at the End of Life* (ANA, 2010c), which reinforces the nurse's obligation to promote comfort and to ensure aggressive efforts to relieve pain and suffering. In 2012, ANA released the position statement *Nursing Care and Do Not Resuscitate (DNR) and Allow Natural Death (AND) Decisions*, which stated that "[n]urses must advocate for and play an active role in initiating discussions about DNR with patients, families, and members of the health care team" (ANA, 2012).

In 2004, the National Consensus Project for Quality Palliative Care (NCP) published *Clinical Practice Guidelines for Quality Palliative Care* (subsequently revised in 2009 and 2013). Designed to promote quality, continuity, and consistent high standards, the guidelines state expectations for education, certification, and ongoing education for members of interdisciplinary hospice and palliative teams, of which registered nurses (RNs) and advanced practice registered nurses (APRNs) are prominent members (NCP, 2013). In 2006, the guidelines served as the foundation of the National Quality Forum's *A National Framework and Preferred Practices for Palliative and Hospice Care: A Consensus Report* (2006), and in 2011 became the underlying principles of The Joint Commission's Advanced Certification in Palliative Care. The 2007 *Hospice and Palliative Nursing: Scope and Standards of Practice* reflected the evolution of palliative care (HPNA & ANA, 2007; ANA, 2010a).

Significant events of the past few years include the recognition of palliative care as a medical specialty, the inclusion of palliative care in healthcare reform, a focus on palliative care as a measurement of quality in national initiatives, and nursing's participation in promoting quality health care. Of particular importance is the 2010 IOM *Future of Nursing* report (IOM, 2010), which identifies rich areas for palliative nursing to grow: the promotion of further education for generalist hospice and palliative nurses to become advanced practice registered nurses; the support of advanced practice registered nurses to practice to the fullest extent to promote universal access to palliative care; and palliative nursing's participation in healthcare quality measures to improve end-of-life care. This revision of *Palliative Nursing: Scope and Standards of Practice* reflects the current state of palliative care and the role of hospice and palliative nurses.

Chronology of Palliative Care and Palliative Nursing Practice, 1986–2013

1986   Hospice Nurses Association (HNA) founded.

1991   American Nurses Association releases *Position Statement: Nursing and the Patient Self-Determination Act—Supporting Autonomy*.

1993   National Board for Certification of Hospice Nursing (NBCHN) established.

1994   National Board for Certification of Hospice Nursing offers first examination for hospice nursing awarding the credential CRNH (Certified Registered Nurse Hospice).
        Physician Orders for Life Sustaining Treatment (POLST) produced in Oregon.

1995   *Standards of Hospice Nursing Practice and Professional Performance* written.
        Study to Understand Prognoses and Preferences for Outcomes and Risks of Treatments (SUPPORT) study released.

1997   Institute of Medicine (IOM) End-of-Life Committee publishes *Approaching Death: Improving Care at the End of Life*.
        Last Acts (a RWJF-funded organization) publishes *The Precepts of Palliative Care*.

1998   Hospice Nurses Association expanded to become the Hospice and Palliative Nurses Association (HPNA).
        The National Board for Certification of Hospice Nursing likewise changes its name to the National Board for Certification of Hospice and Palliative Nurses (NBCHPN®).

American Association of Colleges of Nursing publishes *Peaceful Death: Recommended Competencies and Curricular Guidelines for End-of-Life Nursing Care.*

1999   Certification for registered nurses expanded to include palliative care, and successful candidates are now awarded the credential CHPN® (Certified Hospice and Palliative Nurse).

Establishment of Nursing Leadership Academy for End-of-Life Care to design an agenda for end-of-life care for the nursing profession.

2000   Hospice and Palliative Nurses Association releases *Statement on the Scope and Standards of Hospice and Palliative Nursing Practice.*

Institute of Medicine (IOM) End-of-Life Committee releases: (1) *When Children Die: Improving Palliative and End-of-Life Care for Children and Their Families,* and (2) *Crossing the Quality Chasm: A New Health System for the 21st Century.*

2001   Hospice and Palliative Nurses Association produces *Professional Competencies for the Generalist Hospice and Palliative Nurse.*

White Paper, *Advanced Practice Nurses Role in Palliative Care: A Position Statement from American Nursing Leaders* published.

2002   *Scope and Standards of Hospice and Palliative Nursing Practice* published in collaboration with the American Nurses Association.

Hospice and Palliative Nurses Association produces *Competencies for the Advanced Practice Hospice and Palliative Care Nurse.*

The CHPN® examination is awarded accreditation by the American Board of Nursing Specialties (ABNS).

2003   *HPNA Position Statement—Value of the Professional Nurse in End-of-Life Care* (revised in 2008 and 2011 and name changed to *Value of Professional Nurse in Palliative Care*).

National certification for advanced practice nurses administered by NBCHPN® in partnership with American Nurses Credentialing Center (ANCC).

NBCHPN® initiates the development of a hospice and palliative certification examination for the licensed practical/vocational nurse (LP/VN) with the first national administration for CHPLN® (Certified Hospice and Palliative Licensed Nurse). Accreditation received from the National Commission for Certifying Agencies (NCCA).

2004   *HPNA Position Statement—Value of Nursing Certification* (revised 2009 and 2012 with name change to *Value of Hospice and Palliative Nursing Certification*).

NBCHPN® acquires the hospice and palliative advanced practice exam. Eligible nurse practitioners and clinical nurse specialists are awarded the credential of ACHPN® (Advanced Certified Hospice and Palliative Nurse).

Certification offered for nursing assistants with credential of CHPNA® (Certified Hospice and Palliative Nursing Assistant).

National Consensus Project for Quality Palliative Care Clinical Practice releases *Clinical Practice Guidelines, 1st Edition.*

2006   *HPNA Position Statement—Value of the Advanced Practice Nurse in Palliative Care* (revised 2010 with name changed to *Value of the Advanced Practice Registered Nurse in Palliative Care*).

2007   HPNA and ANA release fourth edition of *Hospice and Palliative Nursing: Scope and Standards of Practice.*

HPNA convenes first Clinical Practice Forum for hospice and palliative nursing.

The ACHPN® exam is awarded accreditation by the ABNS.

2008   Hospice and Palliative Certification is offered for the hospice and palliative care administrator credentialed as CHPCA® (Certified Hospice and Palliative Care Administrator).

2009   *HPNA Position Statement—Assuring High Quality in Hospice and Palliative Nursing* (revised in 2013 with name changed to *Assuring High Quality in Palliative Nursing*).

National Consensus Project for Quality Palliative Care releases *Clinical Practice Guidelines, 2nd Edition.*

2011   *HPNA Position Statement—The Nurse's Role in Advance Care Planning* is released.

First examination for hospice and palliative pediatric nurses offered with credential of CHPPN®.

2013   First interdisciplinary examination for perinatal loss professionals offered with credential of CPLC® (Certified in Perinatal Loss Care).

National Consensus Project for Quality Palliative Care Clinical Practice releases *Clinical Practice Guidelines, 3rd Edition.*

Institute of Medicine (IOM) forms "Transforming Care at the End-of-Life" committee to review and expand palliative care across healthcare settings.

Ethics

Ethics are intrinsic to palliative nursing—concerning the patient, the family, the nurse, and other healthcare providers in the circle of care. In particular, the ethical principles of beneficence, respect for individuals and self-determination, justice, and nonmaleficence, as well as awareness of conflicts of interests, may pertain in the delivery of palliative care (NCP, 2013). Ever-present ethical issues include decision-making capacity; surrogate decision-making in advance care planning; the appropriateness of complex treatments; a patient's right to decline treatments; use of high-dose medications; withdrawal of technology; palliative sedation; futile care; and cessation of hydration and/or artificial and oral nutrition (NCP, 2013). The nine provisions of the *Code of Ethics for Nurses* (ANA, 2001) have specific relevance to palliative nursing:

1. The nurse, in all professional relationships, practices with compassion and respect for the inherent dignity, worth, and uniqueness of every individual, unrestricted by considerations of social or economic status, personal attributes, or the nature of health problems.

As stated in the HPNA *Position Statement: The Nurse's Role in Advance Care Planning* (HPNA, 2011b), the hospice and palliative nurse plays a critical advocacy, educational, and supportive role in a patient's right to self-determination, autonomy, and dignity. Recognizing the diversity in personal, religious, and cultural value systems, the hospice and palliative nurse develops respectful relationships with patients, families, and colleagues. This rapport affords hospice and palliative nurses the unique role of facilitating care throughout the illness trajectory, including providing information about treatment options and advance care planning, which captures the patients' values, preferences, and beliefs. This necessitates the creation of an emotionally safe community: specifically, a culture that accepts reaching out, identifying individual needs, and taking time out. In addition, a physical environment for safe practice, with appropriate guidelines and safeguards, is vital (Vachon & Huggard, 2010).

2. The nurse's primary commitment is to the patient, whether an individual, family, group, or community.

Due to the complexity of care, different perspectives and values may challenge the hospice and palliative nurse's professional values. Although the hospice and palliative nurse's primary responsibility is to the patient and the patient's needs, there is simultaneous accountability to an employer, the nursing profession, fellow colleagues, and the public. Moreover, the nature of early palliative care creates longer-term patient/family associations. These professional relationships have the potential to transform into friendships; enhanced by communication via social media. Therefore, long-term associations require attention to prevent potential overinvolvement or blurring of professional boundaries.

3. The nurse promotes, advocates for, and strives to protect the health, safety, and rights of the patient.

Palliative nursing involves basic patient rights related to safe practice, information sharing, and confidentiality. Maintaining confidentiality is of the utmost importance; the nurse must utilize sound ethical principles in maintaining patient health and personal information. Frequently, a patient reveals sensitive information such as emotions, thoughts, concerns, personal stories (e.g., difficult past history, traumas, abuse), and/or regrets. The principles of privacy shape patient rights about what and with whom information can be shared. Permission to share information, except in emergency situations, is requisite. The hospice and palliative nurse must clearly describe and explain what information is mandated to be shared, why it must be shared, and with whom it will be shared.

4. The nurse is responsible and accountable for individual nursing practices and determines the appropriate delegation of tasks consistent with the nurse's obligations to provide optimal patient care.

It is essential that the hospice and palliative nurse maintain current knowledge within the specialty, as it pertains to individual practice. This is achieved by professional development, particularly through the numerous multimedia educational opportunities and educational forums offered by the Hospice and Palliative Nurses Association. An important practice issue is that the hospice and palliative RN and APRN understand the accountability for and appropriate delegation of nursing activities provided by licensed practical/vocational nurses and nursing assistants under her or his direction. Specifically, the nurse must ensure that in her or his absence, delegated assignments can be competently performed in the diverse settings of palliative care delivery.

5. The nurse owes the same duties to self as to others, including the responsibility to preserve integrity and safety, to maintain competence, and to continue personal and professional growth.

Hospice and palliative nurses attend to patients with difficult pain and symptoms using a range of interventions: high-dose opioids; medications normally reserved for intensive care units within general care units; withdrawal of technology (e.g., ventilators, noninvasive oxygen, pressors, antibiotics, dialysis, artificial nutrition and hydration); and palliative sedation. Therefore, it is essential that policies and procedures exist for safe and ethically sound practice. Nonetheless, even with appropriate processes in place, the many aspects of palliative nursing are subject to differing interpretations of acceptable and relevant palliative practices by members of the circle of care. In all situations, the nurse has the privilege to acknowledge and thoughtfully express her or his moral opinion. When conflict occurs, the nurse may express her or his objection and attempt to resolve the conflict, avoiding both patient abandonment and/or compromised personal values.

6. The nurse participates in establishing, maintaining, and improving health care environments and conditions of employment conducive to the provision of quality health care and consistent with the values of the profession through individual and collective action.

Palliative care is, by its very nature, an interdisciplinary service, with nurses as core members of palliative care teams. The organizational mission and philosophy dictate the culture, environment, and quality of care. Standards of care, practice guidelines, and regulatory standards are all valuable tools that can be employed; while at the same time meeting the nurse's obligation to assure a safe and ethical work environment for all members of the team. Hospice and palliative nurses have a responsibility to influence and contribute to the ethical environment of the organization in clinical practice and employee performance.

7. The nurse participates in the advancement of the profession through contributions to practice, education, administration, and knowledge development.

Palliative nursing has developed and matured; as evidenced by formal educational programs, the presence of hospice and palliative nurses in administration of new and established programs, and its influence in health care policy. Palliative nursing has a prominent role in the state of the art and science of palliative care, as evidenced by leadership in the National Hospice and Palliative Care Coalition, the National Consensus Project for Quality Palliative Care's *Clinical Practice Guidelines*, and the National Quality Forum's palliative measures and outcomes development. Hospice and palliative nurses must continue to create educational and research programs contributing to evidence-based palliative nursing, share and participate in quality improvement process initiatives, and promote access to quality care through legislation, as delineated in the HPNA *Position Statement: Assuring High Quality Palliative Care* (HPNA, 2013).

8. The nurse collaborates with other health professionals and the public in promoting community, national, and international efforts to meet health needs.

Palliative nursing is uniquely positioned to enhance public awareness of and access to palliative care in local, national, and international communities and settings. Examples include pain and symptom management initiatives, care of populations with progressive chronic conditions (e.g., cancer, human immunodeficiency virus [HIV], tuberculosis [TB], heart disease, and pulmonary disease), advance directive programs, direct care and bereavement care during and after disasters, and international palliative nursing education. Hospice and palliative nurses' community initiatives can address barriers to care and improve available services.

9. The profession of nursing, as represented by associations and their members, is responsible for articulating nursing values, for maintaining the integrity of the profession and its practice, and for shaping social policy.

The Hospice and Palliative Nurses Association is the collaborative and visionary professional palliative nursing organization. A unique membership organization with individual membership levels for all members of the nursing team, HPNA offers palliative nursing resources to ensure quality nursing through evidence-based research and educational tools. The resources include education in managing complex physical, psychological, spiritual, and emotional symptoms, along with education on grief and bereavement and instruction in palliative care communication. These resources allow hospice and palliative nurses to engage in important activities, including, but not limited to, educating and training fellow healthcare providers, families, and the public about palliative care and hospice philosophy; influencing palliative nursing through leadership and research; and collaborating with policy-makers, legislators, and insurers to improve coverage of and access to palliative care.

The nature of palliative care involves inherent stress and emotional demands. From the outset, palliative nursing involves providing care that other healthcare providers are uncomfortable or unfamiliar with, in a death-denying society. Caring for patients with serious or life-threatening illness results in constant exposure to crisis, loss, dying, and death. Influences stemming from social norms, culture, spirituality/religion, ethnicity, and country of origin are revealed in the diversity of patients, families, and healthcare professionals; necessitating constant discussion and negotiation. Variable team dynamics and the pressures of the overall healthcare system can further complicate the environment in which the hospice and palliative nurse works. Therefore, hospice and palliative nurses must employ a variety of self-care strategies to promote resiliency and prevent compassion fatigue (Vachon & Huggard, 2010; Mazanec, 2011).

Current State of Practice

Palliative care has matured from a theoretical philosophy into a specialty that continues to evolve; in doing so, it is building a more comprehensive evidence base. It has a growing presence, demonstrated by the fact that in 2012, 67% of hospitals have inpatient palliative care programs, an increase from 24.5% in 2000 (Center to Advance Palliative Care [CAPC], 2013). Since late 2011, The Joint Commission (2012) has offered Advanced Certification for Palliative Care programs for specialist hospital-based programs. A wide range of pediatric, adult, rural, and academic hospitals have attained this certification. Additionally, approximately 1.54 million patients receive hospice care provided by more than 5,500 hospices each year in the United States (National Hospice and Palliative Care Organization [NHPCO], 2013). This is especially significant given the continuing impact of an aging population with serious or life-threatening illness upon health care delivery. As a result, both society and payers are demanding improved attention and care to this population. In the next few years, the palliative care model will move into primary care as a result of current research demonstrating that palliative care decreases hospitalizations and promotes better care.

In the United States, unlike other countries, the Medicare hospice benefit (MHB) has relegated hospice care to the last six months of life (Centers for Medicare and Medicare Services [CMS], 2012). Within the Hospice Conditions of Participation (COPs), the Centers for Medicare and Medicaid Services (CMS) delineates eligibility requirements for the Medicare hospice benefit: a terminal diagnosis with an estimated prognosis of six months or less should the disease take its normal course, and the election of the MHB by the patient and/or family. The COPs describe covered services, which include core services such as nursing, personal care, social work, spiritual care, and physician visits, as well as provision of equipment and medicine necessary for treatment of the terminal condition.

Hospice services are also available from insurance sources other than the MHB. In many states, Medicaid provides a hospice benefit similar to the Medicare hospice benefit. The U.S. Department of Veterans Affairs (VA) provides hospice services through the many VA organizations (e.g., hospitals, state veterans' homes), or contracts hospice services through local hospice providers. Many private or commercial insurances cover hospice services, using guidelines similar to the Medicare hospice benefit. However, there are still insurances that offer no hospice benefits at all.

Palliative care has no specific federal designation as a specialty; rather, it exists as a consultative discipline delivering a philosophy of care. Palliative care clinicians must meet the regulatory requirements for the type of agency under which they deliver palliative care or for the setting in which the palliative care is delivered (e.g., hospital, outpatient or clinic setting, rehabilitation setting, home care, or long-term care).

Palliative Nursing Competencies and Certifications

HPNA "recognizes specialty certification as a mechanism for demonstrating continuing competence" as stated in the HPNA *Position Statement: The Value of Hospice and Palliative Nursing Certification* (HPNA, 2012). The Hospice Nurses Association (HNA) was founded in 1986 as the first professional organization dedicated to promoting excellence in the practice of hospice nursing. The National Board for the Certification of Hospice Nurses (NBCHN) was created in 1993 to offer hospice certification. In 1999, NBCHN added palliative care to its title and became the National Board for Certification of Hospice and Palliative Nurses (NBCHPN®) to assure competence within palliative nursing (NBCHPN®, 2012).

The first examination measuring basic competence in palliative nursing for both hospice and palliative registered nurses was offered in 2001. In 2002, certification for hospice and palliative nursing assistants (CHPNA®) was offered, making NBCHPN® the first organization to certify nursing assistants in a nursing specialty. A 1998 role delineation study, commissioned by the National Board for Certification of Hospice Nurses and subsequently repeated, supported a joint examinclusive of both hospice and palliative nurses (Fabrey & Chuang, 2011). The Certified Hospice and Palliative Nurse (CHPN®) designation is awarded to the registered nurse or the advanced practice registered nurse who is not in the clinical setting.

Advanced practice hospice and palliative nurse certification (now known as Advanced Certified Hospice and Palliative Nurse or ACHPN®) and the certification for licensed practice/vocational nurse (Certified Hospice and Palliative Licensed Nurse®) became available in 2003. In 2011, the examinations for Certified Hospice and Palliative Pediatric Nurse (CHPPN®) and the Certified Hospice and Palliative Care Administrator (CHPCA®) were added. Certification in perinatal loss (CPLC®) for all disciplines is offered as of 2013.

The number of credentialed nurses in palliative care is over 13,900; this does not include certified licensed practical/vocational nurses, nursing assistants, or administrators. With the aging population comes a higher prevalence of progressive, chronic conditions, or life-limiting illnesses. As a result, there will be a proportionate need for more palliative care specialty certified nurses.

Professional Development in Palliative Nursing

As the specialty of palliative nursing evolves, so does the knowledge, competence, and leadership of nurses practicing across the lifespan and in myriad settings. Nurses at the registered nurse and advanced practice levels have a professional and ethical obligation to themselves, the profession, and the public to develop and maintain competence in this area. Specialty professional development within the four pillars of excellence is enriched through HPNA membership with access to a wealth of resources: advocacy in legislation and policy; research and scholarship on clinical outcomes; and continuing education opportunities (e.g., national and regional conferences, e-learning, journals, and textbooks). Competence, via palliative specialty certification, is the ongoing commitment of a registered nurse to integrate and apply the knowledge, skills, and judgment with the attitudes, values, and beliefs required to practice safely, effectively, and ethically in a designated role and setting (NBCHPN®, 2011).

Primary Nursing Practice

Because palliative care is embedded in nursing practice, all nurses practice primary palliative care. This is inherent in the definition of nursing: alleviation of suffering through the diagnosis and treatment of human response, and advocacy in the care of individuals, families, communities, and populations. By the nature of their role, all nurses provide psychosocial support. They have the skills to assess and assist advance care planning, promote illness understanding, and identify spiritual issues and cultural concerns.

Many undergraduate programs offer specific courses in palliative care or incorporate elements of palliative nursing into required classes. These include the essential areas necessary for palliative nursing: self-awareness and compassion; sensitivity to death and dying; strong communication skills with patients, families, and interdisciplinary colleagues; keen assessment skills; and the ability to devise and implement evidence-based plans. Nurses also learn basic pain and symptom management and can promote effective discharge planning. After graduating from an accredited nursing program, registered nurses at the generalist level will have passed the National Council Licensure Examination for Registered Nurses (NCLEX-RN), which includes palliative care content while fulfilling state licensure requirements. At places of employment, orientation and ongoing education programs support nurses' further education and practice in these areas.

Registered Nurse Palliative Nursing Specialty Practice

Registered nurse palliative nursing specialty practice varies according to educational preparation and level of practice, but should reflect the scope and standards of palliative nursing delineated in this document. There is no prescribed preparation for a nurse to become a hospice and palliative registered nurse, because all nurses utilize principles of primary palliative care as the basis of their practice. Nurses who are interested in palliative nursing specialty practice can seek out some of the many available educational resources to gain specific knowledge and skills. This is essential because hospice and palliative registered nurses are expected to have a higher competence in pain and symptom management, communication skills, and coordination of interdisciplinary care. They are able to provide care to patients requiring more complex palliative care.

New graduates and nurses transitioning into hospice and palliative care teams often receive an organizational orientation and professional education to obtain competence in all aspects of the palliative nursing specialty. Registered nurses who choose this career path can undergo specialized training courses, seek out education from HPNA, participate in ELNEC trainings, and develop programs based on the HPNA competencies and NCP guidelines. HPNA provides a plethora of professional educational opportunities for the generalist hospice and palliative nurse, including core curricula (e.g., registered nurse, pediatric, long-term care, and administrator), publications (e.g., competencies, clinical topics, and ethical issues), e-learning courses, conferences, and scholarly research through the *Journal of Hospice and Palliative Nursing*. Their specialty competence will be demonstrated through hospice and palliative nursing certification. It is expected that, throughout their own educational development, hospice and palliative nurses will educate and mentor fellow nurses, other healthcare professionals, and the public on the value of palliative care, particularly its positive impact upon quality of life through advocacy of patient preferences of care, pain and symptom management, psychological support, discharge planning, and bereavement support.

Advanced Practice Palliative Nursing Practice

There are two roles in advanced practice palliative nursing practice. One advanced practice role is that of the graduate-level prepared specialty nurse educated at the master's or doctoral level. Graduate-level prepared specialty nurses are essential to advance palliative care in roles other than direct care provision (e.g., education, research, administration). These nurses practice in a variety of settings, including, but not limited to, academic medical centers, schools of nursing, specialty clinics, community settings, academic research or education settings, and various professional organizations. They promote educational programs in palliative care, all aspects of palliative care and palliative nursing research, and diverse programs for the public, insurers, and international communities. Though not eligible for advanced certification in hospice and palliative nursing, specialty hospice and palliative certification is encouraged. There are examinations for the registered nurse, administrator, pediatric nurse, and perinatal loss expert.

The second, more common role of advanced practice palliative nursing practice is that of the advanced practice registered nurse (APRN). In this document, the title *advanced practice registered nurse (APRN)* is an inclusive term utilized to describe the common core of knowledge, skills, and abilities of nurses clinically educated at the master's-degree level or above, who specialize and practice in palliative nursing. As delineated by the 2008

Consensus Model for APRN Regulation: Licensure, Accreditation, Certification, and Education (LACE) document (APRN Consensus Work Group & National Council of State Boards of Nursing [NCSBN] APRN Advisory Committee, 2008; NCSBN APRN Advisory Committee, 2008), the APRN is a registered nurse (RN) educated at the master's, post-master's, or doctoral level in one of four roles: a clinical nurse specialist (CNS), nurse practitioner (NP), certified nurse midwife (CNM), or certified registered nurse anesthetist (CRNA). Most hospice and palliative APRNs are CNSs and/or NPs. Nurse anesthetists and nurse midwives working in palliative care may practice in areas such as pain management or perinatal palliative care.

All APRNs have the knowledge, skills, abilities, and competency to perform all aspects of basic palliative nursing. However, additional graduate education and preparation enable practice at an advanced level. More graduate programs now include population-focused palliative care education. A number of graduate nursing programs offer dual specialization. This includes primary specialization in one of six nursing population foci as required by LACE (family/individual across the lifespan, adult-gerontology, pediatrics, neonatal, women's health/gender-related, or psychiatric/mental health), as well as the subspecialty of palliative nursing (APRN Consensus Work Group & NCSBN, 2008). There are also more than 10 specialized post-master's-degree palliative care certificate programs. These programs often offer courses, such as pain education, pharmacology, and symptom management for patients with serious or life-threatening illness.

The advanced practice hospice and palliative registered nurse responds to the individual, professional, and societal needs related to the experience of serious or life-threatening illness through the nursing process. APRNs are distinguished by their ability to synthesize complex data, develop and implement advanced plans, and provide leadership in hospice and palliative nursing. Roles of APRNs in hospice and palliative nursing include, but are not limited to:

- Expert clinician

- Leader of interdisciplinary teams

- Educator

- Researcher

- Consultant

- Collaborator

- Advocate

- Case manager

- Administrator

- Program developer

- Policy-maker

APRNs, having fulfilled established requirements of their state nurse practice act, regulations, or statutes, may be authorized to assume autonomous responsibility for clinical role functions. Their roles may include the prescription of medications, controlled substances, or therapies. National certification in advanced practice palliative nursing is recommended for APRNs in this specialty.

Beyond requirements for licensure, it is essential that both graduate-level prepared specialty nurses and APRNs participate in lifelong continuing education regarding palliative care, policy issues, and industry trends. Sources of education are similar to those listed in the RN section; there are also education offerings targeted to their advanced role.

Palliative Nursing Competencies

The competencies in palliative nursing summarized in this section represent the knowledge, skills, and abilities demonstrated when providing evidence-based physical, emotional, psychosocial, and spiritual care necessary for the registered nurse, graduate-level prepared specialty nurse, and advanced practice registered nurse (HPNA, 2002, 2010). The care is provided in a collaborative manner across the lifespan in diverse settings to patients and families experiencing serious or life-threatening illness.

CLINICAL JUDGMENT

The hospice and palliative nurse demonstrates critical thinking, analysis, and clinical judgment in all aspects of palliative care. The hospice and palliative nurse cares for patients with myriad conditions related to neurology, cardiology, pulmonary, oncology, nephrology, gastroenterology, hepatology, dementias, endocrinology, and infectious disease. Using the nursing process, the hospice and palliative nurse addresses the physical, psychosocial, emotional, and spiritual needs of patients and families. Clinical judgment is demonstrated in the provision of effective pain and symptom management.

ADVOCACY AND ETHICS

The hospice and palliative nurse incorporates ethical principles and professional standards in the care of patients and families experiencing serious or life-threatening illness. The hospice and palliative nurse provides patient-centered care through the identification of and advocacy for patient and family values, wishes, and preferences of care; promotes ethical and legal decision-making; and improves access to care and community resources by influencing or formulating health and social policy.

PROFESSIONALISM

The hospice and palliative nurse demonstrates knowledge, attitudes, behaviors, and skills that are consistent with palliative nursing professional standards, codes of ethics, and scope of practice. Examples of professionalism include:

- Contributing to improved quality and cost-effectiveness of palliative care services.

- Participating in the generation, testing, and evaluation of palliative care knowledge and practice.

- Participating in professional palliative care organizations.

- Obtaining certification.

COLLABORATION

As described in the definition, the nature of palliative care is collaborative. The hospice and palliative nurse actively promotes communication and collaboration among patients, families, and the interdisciplinary team. Through collaborative practice, the hospice and palliative nurse engages with other nursing specialties (e.g., wound ostomy nurses, oncology, nutritional support, case management), healthcare team members, and the community to address and plan for issues related to living with and dying from a serious or life-threatening illness.

SYSTEMS THINKING

The hospice and palliative nurse identifies and utilizes system resources necessary to enhance the quality of life for patients and families experiencing serious or life-threatening illness. The hospice and palliative nurse integrates system thinking into comprehensive care delivery and quality initiatives within healthcare organizations. This is particularly significant in healthcare reform, where organizations are being challenged to provide care appropriate to patient wishes and reduce hospital readmission rates. Hospice and palliative nurses can participate in creative implementation of primary palliative care in accountable care organizations and patient medical homes. Their roles will include the development of community programs such as advance care planning, home visits to frail elders, and presence in primary care clinics to collaborate with colleagues.

CULTURAL COMPETENCE

Cultural competence refers to the process by which hospice and palliative nurses respond respectfully and effectively to people of all cultures and languages, while recognizing and affirming the unique values of the patient, family, and the interdisciplinary team members within a community (NCP, 2013). The hospice and palliative nurse elicits cultural identification, including perceptions related to family composition, illness, treatment, decision-making, death, and dying. In addition, the nurse addresses the multidimensional psychosocial and spiritual needs of patients and families from diagnosis through death. Cultural values and rituals are incorporated into the plan.

FACILITATION OF LEARNING

The hospice and palliative nurse creates opportunities and initiatives for palliative care education for patients, families, colleagues, and the community. This is accomplished through development, implementation, and evaluation of formal and informal education related to living with and dying from serious or life-threatening illness.

COMMUNICATION

The hospice and palliative nurse uses effective verbal, nonverbal, and written communication with patients and families, members of the interdisciplinary team, and the community. Therapeutic communication skills are utilized to accurately convey and therapeutically address the palliative needs of patients and families throughout the palliative care continuum. An essential feature of the communication process is cultural competence, particularly the mandatory use of interpreters when patients and families do not speak or understand English, or feel more comfortable communicating in a language other than English (NCP, 2013). Addressing numeracy and literacy (i.e., cognitive, educational, health, and financial) is fundamental (NCP, 2013). Precise written and verbal communication in one's language of preference is vital, especially during transitions of care.

Summary

Palliative nursing is a specialty with its own art and science unlimited by body system, diagnosis, prognosis, setting, or age. It is applicable to any patient with serious or life-threatening illness or injury upon diagnosis, and to the patient's family. Patient and family values, preferences, and goals establish the basis for creation of the plan. Hospice and palliative nurses attend to the holistic care of the patient and family, inclusive of their physical, psychosocial, emotional, and spiritual needs. Care includes support of the family (as defined by the patient), first as caregivers and then as bereaved persons after the patient dies. Hospice and palliative nurses use their knowledge of and expertise in palliative care to collaborate with other interdisciplinary team members and promote access to available resources.

Standards of Palliative Nursing Practice

The standards of palliative nursing practice are authoritative statements developed by the Hospice and Palliative Nurses Association for the nursing profession and the public. The standards identify the responsibilities for which hospice and palliative nurses are accountable. They may be used as evidence of the standard of care, with the understanding that application of the standards is context dependent. The standards reflect the values and priorities of palliative nursing and provide a framework for the evaluation of practice. The standards are written in measurable terms, defining hospice and palliative nurses' accountability to the public, and describing obtainable patient and family outcomes.

The standards are divided into two sections: the Standards of Practice and the Standards of Professional Performance. Each standard identifies competencies that may be evidence of compliance with the corresponding standard. The standards remain stable over time, reflecting the philosophical values of the profession. To be consistent with current nursing practice and reflect evidence-based practices; the competencies are periodically revised to incorporate advancements in scientific knowledge, technology, and clinical practice.

Standards of Practice

Standards of Practice describe a competent level of registered and advanced practice registered nursing care, as demonstrated by the nursing process:

- Assessment

- Diagnosis

- Outcomes identification

- Planning

- Implementation (determined by level of practice, licensure, and regulatory standards of practice; may include coordination of care, health teaching and health promotion, consultation, and prescriptive authority and treatment)

■ Evaluation

Standards of Professional Performance

Standards of Professional Performance and the associated measurement criteria describe competent professional role behaviors, including activities related to:

■ Ethics

■ Education

■ Evidence-based practice and research

■ Quality of practice

■ Communication

■ Leadership

■ Collaboration

■ Professional practice evaluation

■ Resource utilization

■ Environmental health

Standards of Practice for Palliative Nursing

Standard 1. Assessment

The hospice and palliative registered nurse collects comprehensive data pertinent to the patient's health and/or the situation.

COMPETENCIES

The hospice and palliative registered nurse:

- Collects data to create a comprehensive history, including, but not limited to, chief complaint, history of present illness, past medical/surgical history, family history, social history, functional status, immunization history, allergies, and palliative review of systems.

- Assesses functional, psychosocial, emotional, cognitive, sexual, cultural, age-related, environmental, spiritual/transpersonal, and economic aspects of care in a systematic and ongoing process while honoring the uniqueness of the patient as a person.

- Determines the patient and family's emotional response and coping in respect to advanced illness, anticipatory grief, complicated grief, depression, anxiety, and delirium (NCP, 2013).

- Evaluates the social aspects in the patient's care, in particular the social well-being, coping skills, educational needs, family dynamics, and goals of each patient and family, as appropriate to the health care setting and the presence of other interdisciplinary team (NCP, 2013). Considers impact on the patient's health, wellness, and illness, as well as death and dying.

- Elicits the patient's values, preferences, beliefs, expressed needs, and understanding of his or her condition.

- Involves the patient, family, and other healthcare providers as appropriate, in holistic data collection.

- Identifies barriers (e.g., psychosocial, literacy, language, financial, cultural) to effective communication and makes appropriate adaptations.

- Recognizes the impact of personal attitudes, values, and beliefs on palliative care delivery.

- Assesses the spiritual/religious/existential realm depending on the patient's beliefs, including, but not limited to, the meaning of illness, life, and death; a connectedness to self, others, nature, a spiritual being and/or God; a sense of hope/hopelessness; and/or a need for forgiveness, as appropriate to the healthcare setting and the presence of other interdisciplinary team members (NCP, 2013).

- Prioritizes data collection based on the patient's immediate condition, or the anticipated needs of the patient, family, or situation.

- Uses appropriate evidence-based assessment techniques, instruments, and tools (e.g., pain scales, functional assessment tools, physical and psychiatric symptom scales, quality-of-life rating scales, prognostic scales).

- Synthesizes available data, information, and knowledge relevant to the situation to identify patterns and variances.

- Applies ethical, legal, and privacy guidelines and policies to the collection, maintenance, use, and dissemination of data and information.

- Recognizes patients as the authority on their own health by honoring their care preferences.

- Documents relevant data in a retrievable format.

ADDITIONAL COMPETENCIES FOR THE GRADUATE-LEVEL PREPARED SPECIALTY NURSE AND THE APRN

The hospice and palliative graduate-level prepared specialty nurse or the advanced practice registered nurse:

- Initiates and interprets diagnostic tests and procedures relevant to the patient's current status.

- Assesses the effectiveness of interactions among patients, family, community, and social systems on health and illness.

- Reviews allergies and current medication for maximum effectiveness and possible need for adjustment based on further assessments.

Standard 2. Diagnosis

The hospice and palliative registered nurse analyzes the assessment data to determine the patient's diagnoses or issues.

COMPETENCIES

The hospice and palliative registered nurse:

- Derives diagnoses or issues from assessment data related to palliative care.

- Validates the diagnoses, problems, or concerns with the patient, family, and the interdisciplinary team, as well as other healthcare providers and caregivers, when possible and appropriate.

- Identifies actual or potential risks to the patient's health and safety or barriers to health, which may include, but are not limited to, interpersonal, systemic, or environmental circumstances.

- Uses standardized classification systems and clinical decision support tools, when available, in identifying palliative diagnoses and illness trajectories.

- Documents palliative diagnoses or issues in a manner that facilitates the determination of the expected outcomes and plan.

ADDITIONAL COMPETENCIES FOR THE GRADUATE-LEVEL PREPARED SPECIALTY NURSE AND THE APRN

The hospice and palliative graduate-level prepared specialty nurse or the advanced practice registered nurse:

- Systematically compares and contrasts clinical findings with normal and abnormal variations and developmental events in formulating a differential diagnosis.

- Utilizes complex data and information obtained during interview, examination, diagnostic procedures and processes, and family meetings in identifying palliative diagnoses.

- Assists staff in developing and maintaining competency in the diagnostic process.

Standard 3. Outcomes Identification

The hospice and palliative registered nurse identifies, in partnership with the interdisciplinary health care team, expected outcomes for a plan individualized to the patient or the situation.

COMPETENCIES

The hospice and palliative registered nurse:

- Identifies the goals of care as stated by the patient, surrogate, health-care proxy, or as documented through advance care planning (NCP, 2013).

- Involves and collaborates with the patient, family, interdisciplinary team, and others while formulating expected outcomes to improve quality of life.

- Derives culturally, developmentally, and age-appropriate expected outcomes based on goals of care, the diagnoses, and health status.

- Considers associated risks, benefits, costs, current scientific evidence, expected trajectory of the condition, and clinical expertise when formulating expected outcomes.

- Defines expected outcomes in terms of the patient and family's goals of care, quality of life, values, culture, and ethical considerations.

- Includes a time estimate for attainment of expected outcomes.

- Develops expected outcomes that provide direction for continuity of care across care settings, from the period of diagnosis through family bereavement.

- Modifies expected outcomes according to situational and status changes of the patient.

- Documents expected outcomes as measurable goals.

**ADDITIONAL COMPETENCIES FOR THE GRADUATE-LEVEL
PREPARED SPECIALTY NURSE AND THE APRN**

The hospice and palliative graduate-level prepared specialty nurse or the advanced practice registered nurse:

■ Identifies expected outcomes that incorporate scientific evidence and are achievable through implementation of evidence-based practices.

■ Identifies expected outcomes that incorporate cost and clinical effectiveness, patient satisfaction, and continuity and consistency among providers.

■ Differentiates outcomes that require process interventions from those that require system-level interventions.

Standard 4. Planning

The hospice and palliative registered nurse develops a plan that defines strategies and alternatives to attain expected outcomes.

COMPETENCIES

The hospice and palliative registered nurse:

- Develops an individualized plan in partnership with the patient, family, and others, with consideration of the person's characteristics or situation. This includes, but is not limited to, health status, quality of life, values, beliefs, spiritual and health practices, preferences, choices, developmental level, coping style, culture and environment, and available technology.

- Establishes the priorities of the plan with the patient and family, in collaboration with the interdisciplinary team and others, as appropriate.

- Includes strategies that address each of the identified diagnoses or issues in the plan. These may include, but are not limited to, strategies for:

  - Promotion, restoration, and/or maintenance of quality of life;

  - Prevention of complications, further illness, injury, and additional disease;

  - Promotion of comfort;

  - Palliation of symptoms and suffering; and

  - Supportive care for patients with serious or life-threatening illness and their families.

- Includes strategies for health and wholeness across the lifespan.

- Provides for continuity in the plan across settings and through the family bereavement.

- Incorporates an implementation pathway or timeline in the plan, including regular family meetings to clarify and reaffirm and/or revise the goals of care.

- Considers the economic impact of the plan on the patient, family, caregivers, or other affected parties.

- Integrates current scientific evidence, trends, and research into palliative care.

- Utilizes the plan to provide direction to and collaborate with other members of the healthcare team.

- Explores potential safe practice settings and space for care delivery. Allows time for the nurse and the patient to explore suggested, potential, and alternative options.

- Defines the plan to reflect current statutes, rules and regulations, and standards.

- Modifies the plan of care according to the ongoing assessment of the patient's health status, response to interventions, and other outcome indicators.

- Documents the plan in a manner that utilizes standardized language or recognized terminology.

- Supports patients and families in advance care planning (e.g., advance directives, living will, and healthcare surrogate decision-makers).

- Promotes financial/business planning (e.g., guardianship, power of attorney for health care, legal power of attorney, wills, and funeral arrangements).

ADDITIONAL COMPETENCIES FOR THE GRADUATE-LEVEL PREPARED SPECIALTY NURSE AND THE APRN

The hospice and palliative graduate-level prepared specialty nurse or the advanced practice registered nurse:

- Identifies assessment strategies, diagnostic strategies, and therapeutic interventions that reflect current evidence, including data, research, literature, and expert clinical knowledge.

- Selects or designs strategies to meet the multifaceted needs of complex patients.

- Includes the synthesis of the patient's and family's values and beliefs regarding nursing and medical therapies in the plan.

- Leads the design and development of interprofessional processes to address the identified diagnosis, problem, or concern.

- Actively participates in the development and continuous improvement of systems that support the planning process.

Standard 5. Implementation

The hospice and palliative registered nurse implements the identified plan.

COMPETENCIES

The hospice and palliative registered nurse:

- Implements a comprehensive physical and mental status examination with respect to appropriate age and developmental needs for patients.

- Partners with the patient, family, significant others, and caregivers as appropriate to implement the plan in a safe, realistic, and timely manner.

- Demonstrates caring behaviors toward patients, families, significant others, and groups of people receiving care.

- Utilizes technology to measure, record, and retrieve patient data; implement the nursing process; and enhance nursing practice.

- Utilizes evidence-based interventions and treatments specific to the diagnosis, disease status, or problem.

- Provides holistic care that addresses the needs of diverse populations across the lifespan.

- Advocates for health care that is sensitive to the needs of patients and relevant to the patient's health status, with particular emphasis on the needs of diverse populations.

- Applies appropriate knowledge of major health problems, illness trajectories, and cultural diversity in implementing the plan.

- Applies available healthcare technologies to maximize access and optimize outcomes for patients.

- Utilizes community resources and systems to implement the plan, as needed.

- Collaborates with healthcare providers from diverse backgrounds to implement and integrate the plan.

- Accommodates different communication styles used by patients, families, and healthcare providers.

- Integrates traditional and complementary health care practices as appropriate.

- Implements the plan in a timely manner in accordance with patient safety goals.

- Promotes the patient's capacity for the optimal level of participation and problem-solving.

- Documents implementation and any modifications, including changes or omissions, of the identified plan.

ADDITIONAL COMPETENCIES FOR THE GRADUATE-LEVEL PREPARED SPECIALTY NURSE AND THE APRN

The hospice and palliative graduate-level prepared specialty nurse or the advanced practice registered nurse:

- Facilitates utilization of systems, organizations, and community resources to implement the plan.

- Supports collaboration with patients, family members, nursing, the palliative care interdisciplinary team, and other colleagues to implement the plan.

- Incorporates new knowledge and strategies to initiate change in nursing practices if desired outcomes are not achieved.

- Assumes responsibility for the safe and efficient implementation of the plan.

- Uses advanced communication skills to promote relationships between nurses and patients, providing a context for open discussion of the patient's experience and to improve patient outcomes.

- Actively participates in the development and continuous improvement of systems that support implementation of the plan.

Standard 5A. Coordination of Care

The hospice and palliative registered nurse coordinates care delivery.

COMPETENCIES

The hospice and palliative registered nurse:

- Organizes the components of the palliative care plan.

- Manages a patient's care so as to maximize independence and promote quality of life.

- Assists the patient to identify options for alternative care.

- Communicates with the patient, family, and clinician colleagues during transitions in care.

- Advocates for the delivery of dignified and humane care by the interdisciplinary team.

- Documents the coordination of the interdisciplinary care within healthcare documentation systems.

ADDITIONAL COMPETENCIES FOR THE GRADUATE-LEVEL PREPARED SPECIALTY NURSE AND THE APRN

The hospice and palliative graduate-level prepared specialty nurse or the advanced practice registered nurse:

- Provides leadership in the coordination of interdisciplinary health care for integrated delivery of patient care services.

- Synthesizes data and information to prescribe necessary system and community support measures, including modifications of surroundings.

Standard 5B. Health Teaching and Health Promotion

The hospice and palliative registered nurse employs strategies to promote health and a safe environment.

COMPETENCIES

The hospice and palliative registered nurse:

- Educates patients and families about decision-making, including promotion of the power of choice in decision-making, especially in serious or life-threatening illness.

- Provides health teaching that addresses such topics as healthy lifestyles, risk-reducing behaviors, developmental needs, activities of daily living, and preventive self-care in the promotion of "living with serious illness."

- Uses health promotion and health teaching methods appropriate to the situation and the patient's values, beliefs, health practices, developmental level, learning needs, readiness, ability to learn, language preference, spirituality, culture, and socioeconomic status.

- Seeks opportunities for feedback and evaluation of the effectiveness of the strategies used.

- Uses information technologies to communicate health promotion and disease prevention information to the patient in a variety of settings.

- Provides patients with information about intended effects and potential adverse effects of proposed therapies.

- Provides patient-centered learning opportunities that focus on enhancing the patient's quality of life.

- Implements community education programs about palliative care such as advance care planning, hospice and palliative services, pain and symptom management, and caring for patients with serious or life-threatening illness.

ADDITIONAL COMPETENCIES FOR THE GRADUATE-LEVEL PREPARED SPECIALTY NURSE AND THE APRN

The hospice and palliative graduate-level prepared specialty nurse or the advanced practice registered nurse:

- Synthesizes empirical evidence on risk behaviors, learning theories, behavioral change theories, motivational theories, epidemiology, and other related theories and frameworks when designing health education information and programs.

- Conducts personalized health teaching and counseling considering comparative effectiveness research recommendations.

- Designs both health information and patient/family education appropriate to the patient's and family's developmental level, learning needs, readiness to learn, and cultural values and beliefs.

- Evaluates health information resources, such as the Internet, in the area of practice for accuracy, readability, and comprehensibility to help patients access quality health information.

- Engages the breadth of consumer groups, public alliances, and advocacy groups, as appropriate, in health teaching and health promotion activities.

- Provides anticipatory guidance to patients, families, groups, and communities both to promote health and prevent or reduce health risks.

Standard 5C. Consultation

The hospice and palliative graduate-level specialty nurse or advanced practice registered nurse provides consultation to influence the identified plan, enhance the abilities of others, and effect change.

COMPETENCIES FOR THE GRADUATE-LEVEL PREPARED SPECIALTY NURSE AND THE APRN

The hospice and palliative graduate-level prepared specialty nurse or the advanced practice registered nurse:

- Synthesizes clinical data, theoretical frameworks, and evidence when providing consultation.

- Facilitates the effectiveness of a consultation by involving the patient, family, and stakeholders in decision-making and negotiation of role responsibilities.

- Communicates consultation recommendations to all team members involved with the patient's care.

Standard 5D. Prescriptive Authority and Treatment

The hospice and palliative advanced practice registered nurse uses prescriptive authority, procedures, referrals, treatments, and therapies in accordance with state and federal laws and regulations.

**COMPETENCIES FOR THE GRADUATE-LEVEL PREPARED
SPECIALTY NURSE AND THE APRN**

The hospice and palliative graduate-level prepared specialty nurse or the advanced practice registered nurse:

- Prescribes evidence-based treatments, therapies, and procedures considering the patient's comprehensive health care needs.

- Prescribes pharmacologic agents based on a current knowledge of pharmacology and physiology.

- Prescribes specific pharmacological agents and treatments based on clinical indicators, the patient's status and needs, and the results of diagnostic and laboratory tests.

- Evaluates therapeutic and potential adverse effects of pharmacological and nonpharmacological treatments.

- Provides patients with information about intended effects and potential adverse effects of proposed prescriptive therapies.

- Provides information about costs and alternative treatments and procedures, as appropriate.

- Evaluates and incorporates complementary and alternative therapy into education and practice.

Standard 6. Evaluation

The hospice and palliative registered nurse evaluates progress towards attainment of outcomes.

COMPETENCIES

The hospice and palliative registered nurse:

- Conducts a systematic, ongoing, and criterion-based evaluation of the outcomes in relation to the structures and processes prescribed by the plan and the indicated timeline.

- Collaborates with the patient, family, and others involved in the care or situation in the evaluative process.

- Evaluates, in partnership with the patient, the effectiveness of the planned strategies in relation to the patient's responses and attainment of the expected outcomes.

- Uses ongoing assessment data to revise the diagnoses, the outcomes, the plan, and the implementation as needed.

- Evaluates outcomes of care of patients and populations to identify opportunities to enhance patient care and outcomes.

- Disseminates the results of the evaluation to the patient, family, interdisciplinary team, and others involved, in accordance with state and federal laws and regulations.

- Participates in assessing and assuring the responsible and appropriate use of interventions. Such interventions are aimed at maximizing quality of life and comfort, while minimizing unwarranted or unwanted treatment and patient suffering.

- Documents the results of the evaluation.

ADDITIONAL COMPETENCIES FOR THE GRADUATE-LEVEL
PREPARED SPECIALTY NURSE AND THE APRN

The hospice and palliative graduate-level prepared specialty nurse or the advanced practice registered nurse:

- Evaluates the accuracy of the diagnosis and effectiveness of the interventions and other variables in relationship to the patient's attainment of expected outcomes.

- Synthesizes the results of the evaluation to determine the effect of the plan on patients, families, groups, communities, and institutions.

- Adapts the plan and treatment trajectory according to the evaluation of response to various interventions.

- Uses the results of the evaluation as part of quality improvement processes to make or recommend process or structural changes, including policy, procedure, or protocol documentation, as appropriate.

Standards of Professional Performance for Palliative Nursing

Standard 7. Ethics

The hospice and palliative registered nurse practices ethically.

COMPETENCIES

The hospice and palliative registered nurse:

- Uses the *Code of Ethics for Nurses with Interpretive Statements* (ANA, 2001) to guide practice.

- Delivers care in a manner that preserves and protects patient autonomy, dignity, rights, values, and beliefs.

- Recognizes the centrality of the patient and family as core members of any healthcare team.

- Upholds the patient's confidentiality within legal and regulatory parameters.

- Assists patients in self-determination and informed decision-making.

- Maintains a therapeutic and professional patient–nurse relationship with appropriate professional role boundaries.

- Contributes to resolving ethical issues involving patients, colleagues, community groups, systems, and other stakeholders.

- Takes appropriate action regarding instances of illegal, unethical, or inappropriate behavior that could endanger or jeopardize the best interests of the patient or situation.

- Questions, when appropriate, healthcare practices and/or addresses issues related to safety and quality improvement.

- Advocates for equitable access to care.

- Articulates a working knowledge of palliative and end-of-life ethical issues.

**ADDITIONAL COMPETENCIES FOR THE GRADUATE-LEVEL
PREPARED SPECIALTY NURSE AND THE APRN**

The hospice and palliative graduate-level prepared specialty nurse or the advanced practice registered nurse:

- Promotes patient care practices that originate from the ethical principles of beneficence, respect for individuals and self-determination, justice, and nonmaleficence, with attention to avoiding conflicts of interest.

- Participates in interdisciplinary teams that address ethical risks, burdens, benefits, and outcomes.

- Provides information on the risks, burdens, benefits, and outcomes of healthcare regimens to allow informed decision-making by the patient, including informed consent, assent, and refusal.

- Initiates ethical review of clinical and healthcare issues.

- Seeks counsel from an ethics committee, as appropriate.

- Maintains knowledge of legal issues in palliative care, such as those related to federal and state law for resuscitation orders, informed consent, a patient's right to decline care, use of high-dose medications, withdrawal of technology (e.g., ventilators, dialysis, antibiotics), palliative sedation, futile care, cessation of artificial and oral nutrition and hydration, and other pertinent issues.

Standard 8. Education

The hospice and palliative registered nurse attains knowledge and competence that reflect current nursing practice.

COMPETENCIES

The hospice and palliative registered nurse:

- Participates in ongoing educational activities related to appropriate knowledge base and professional topics related to palliative care.

- Educates patient, families, other healthcare clinicians, and the public about hospice, palliative care, and the role of the hospice and palliative nurse.

- Demonstrates a commitment to lifelong learning through self-reflection and to address learning needs and professional growth needs.

- Seeks experiences that reflect current palliative nursing practice to maintain knowledge, skills, abilities, and judgment in clinical practice or role performance.

- Acquires palliative knowledge and skills appropriate to her or his role, population, specialty, setting, or situation.

- Seeks formal and independent learning activities to develop and maintain clinical and professional skills and knowledge in palliative nursing.

- Identifies learning needs based on palliative nursing knowledge, the various roles the nurse may assume, and the changing needs of the population.

- Participates in formal and informal consultations to address issues in palliative nursing practice as an application of education and knowledge base.

- Shares educational findings, experiences, and ideas with peers.

- Contributes to a work environment conducive to the education of healthcare professionals.

- Maintains professional records that provide evidence of competence and lifelong learning in palliative nursing.

ADDITIONAL COMPETENCIES FOR THE GRADUATE-LEVEL PREPARED SPECIALTY NURSE AND THE APRN

The hospice and palliative graduate-level prepared specialty nurse or the advanced practice registered nurse:

- Uses current healthcare research findings and other evidence to expand clinical knowledge, skills, abilities, and judgment; to enhance role performance; and to increase knowledge of professional topics.

Standard 9. Evidence-Based Practice and Research

The hospice and palliative registered nurse integrates evidence and research findings into practice.

COMPETENCIES

The hospice and palliative registered nurse:

- Utilizes current evidence-based nursing knowledge, including research findings, to guide palliative nursing practice.

- Incorporates evidence when initiating changes in palliative nursing practice.

- Participates, as appropriate to education level and position, in the formulation of evidence-based practice through research.

- Shares personal or third-party research findings with colleagues and peers.

ADDITIONAL COMPETENCIES FOR THE GRADUATE-LEVEL
PREPARED SPECIALTY NURSE AND THE APRN

The hospice and palliative graduate-level prepared specialty nurse or the advanced practice registered nurse:

- Contributes to nursing knowledge by conducting or synthesizing research and other evidence that discovers, examines, and evaluates current practice, knowledge, theories, criteria, and creative approaches to improve healthcare outcomes.

- Promotes a climate of research and clinical inquiry.

- Disseminates palliative research findings through activities such as presentations, publications, consultation, and journal clubs.

Standard 10. Quality of Practice

The hospice and palliative registered nurse contributes to quality palliative nursing practice.

COMPETENCIES

The hospice and palliative registered nurse:

- Demonstrates quality by documenting the application of the palliative nursing process in a responsible, accountable, and ethical manner.

- Focuses on quality palliative nursing relating to serious or life-threatening illness, offering the right care at the right time, in the course of a patient's disease or condition.

- Uses creativity and innovation to enhance palliative nursing care.

- Leads quality improvement activities, which may include:

  - Identifying aspects of practice important for quality monitoring.

  - Using indicators to monitor quality, safety, and effectiveness of nursing practice.

  - Collecting data to monitor quality and effectiveness of nursing practice.

  - Analyzing quality data to identify opportunities for improving nursing practice.

  - Formulating recommendations to improve nursing practice or outcomes.

  - Implementing activities to enhance the quality of nursing practice and clinical outcomes.

  - Developing, implementing, and/or evaluating policies, procedures, and guidelines to improve the quality of practice.

  - Participating on and/or leading interprofessional teams to evaluate clinical care or health services.

  - Participating in and/or leading efforts to minimize costs and un-necessary duplication of services.

- Identifying problems that occur in day-to-day work routines in order to correct process inefficiencies.*

- Analyzing factors related to quality, safety, and effectiveness.

- Analyzing organizational systems for barriers to quality patient outcomes.

- Implementing processes to remove or weaken barriers within organizational systems.

■ Obtains and maintains professional certification in palliative nursing, as appropriate.

ADDITIONAL COMPETENCIES FOR THE GRADUATE-LEVEL PREPARED SPECIALTY NURSE AND THE APRN

The hospice and palliative graduate-level prepared specialty nurse or the advanced practice registered nurse:

- Provides leadership in the design and implementation of quality improvements within palliative nursing.

- Designs innovations to effect change in practice and improve health outcomes.

- Evaluates the practice environment and quality of palliative nursing care rendered in relation to existing evidence.

- Identifies opportunities for the initiation of and use of research and evidence in palliative nursing.

- Uses the results of quality improvement to initiate changes in palliative nursing practice and health care delivery systems.

---

* Board of Higher Education & Massachusetts Organization of Nurse Executives [BHE/MONE], 2006.

Standard 11. Communication

The hospice and palliative registered nurse communicates effectively in a variety of formats in all areas of practice.

COMPETENCIES

The hospice and palliative registered nurse:

- Demonstrates effective communication skills with the interdisciplinary team, displaying respect for their roles and unique contributions to the care of the patient.

- Assesses communication format preferences of patients, families, and colleagues.*

- Assesses her or his own communication skills in encounters with patients, families, interdisciplinary team, and colleagues.*

- Seeks continuous improvement of her or his own communication and conflict resolution skills.*

- Conveys information to patients, families, the interdisciplinary team, and others in communication formats that are timely, thorough, current, comprehensive, and accurate.

- Questions the rationale supporting care processes and decisions when they do not appear to be in the best interest of the patient.*

- Discloses observations or concerns related to hazards and errors in care or the practice environment to the appropriate level.

- Maintains communication with other providers to minimize risks associated with transfers and transition in care delivery.

- Contributes her or his own professional perspective in discussions with the interdisciplinary team.

- Initiates communication about essential hospice and palliative care issues, such as diagnosis, prognosis, bad news, goals of care, and imminent death.

---

* BHE/MONE, 2006.

Standard 12. Leadership

The hospice and palliative registered nurse demonstrates leadership in the professional practice setting and the profession.

COMPETENCIES

The hospice and palliative registered nurse:

- Oversees the nursing care delegated to other personnel while retaining accountability for the quality of care given to the patient.

- Abides by the vision, the associated goals, and the plan to implement and measure progress of an individual patient or progress within the context of the healthcare organization.

- Demonstrates a commitment to continuous, lifelong learning for self and others.

- Mentors colleagues for the advancement of nursing practice, the profession, and quality health care.

- Treats colleagues with respect, trust, and dignity.*

- Develops communication and conflict resolution skills.

- Participates in professional organizations.

- Communicates effectively with the patient and colleagues.

- Seeks ways to advance nursing autonomy and accountability.*

- Participates in efforts to influence healthcare policy involving patients and the profession.

ADDITIONAL COMPETENCIES FOR THE GRADUATE-LEVEL PREPARED SPECIALTY NURSE AND THE APRN

The hospice and palliative graduate-level prepared specialty nurse or the advanced practice registered nurse:

- Influences decision-making bodies to improve the professional practice environment and patient outcomes.

---

* BHE/MONE, 2006.

■ Provides direction to enhance the effectiveness of the interdisciplinary team and outcomes.

■ Promotes advanced practice nursing and role development by interpreting its role for patients, families, and others.

■ Models expert advanced palliative nursing practice to interdisciplinary team members and patients.

■ Mentors colleagues in the acquisition of clinical knowledge, skills, abilities, and judgment.

Standard 13. Collaboration

The hospice and palliative registered nurse collaborates with patient, family, interdisciplinary team, and others in the conduct of nursing practice.

COMPETENCIES

The hospice and palliative registered nurse:

- Partners with others to effect change and produce positive outcomes through the sharing of knowledge of the patient, family, and/or situation.

- Communicates with the patient, family, interdisciplinary team, and healthcare providers regarding a patient's care and the nurse's role in the provision of that care.

- Promotes conflict management and engagement.

- Participates in building consensus or resolving conflict in the context of patient care.

- Applies group process and negotiation techniques with patients and colleagues.

- Adheres to standards and applicable codes of conduct that govern behavior among peers and colleagues to create a work environment that promotes cooperation, respect, and trust.

- Cooperates in creating a documented plan focused on outcomes and decisions related to care and delivery of services that indicates communication with patients, families, and others.

- Engages in teamwork and team-building processes.

- Documents referrals, including provisions for continuity of care.

ADDITIONAL COMPETENCIES FOR THE GRADUATE-LEVEL PREPARED SPECIALTY NURSE AND THE APRN

The hospice and palliative graduate-level prepared specialty nurse or the advanced practice registered nurse:

- Partners with other disciplines to enhance patient outcomes through interprofessional activities, such as education, consultation, management, technological development, or research opportunities.

- Invites the contributions of the patient, family, and team members in order to achieve optimal outcomes.

- Leads in establishing, improving, and sustaining collaborative relationships to achieve safe quality patient care and enhance system processes.

- Documents palliative plan communications, rationales for plan changes, and collaborative discussions to improve patient care.

Standard 14. Professional Practice Evaluation

The hospice and palliative registered nurse evaluates her or his own nursing practice in relation to professional practice standards and guidelines, relevant statutes, rules, and regulations.

COMPETENCIES

The hospice and palliative registered nurse:

- Provides age and developmentally appropriate care in a culturally and ethnically sensitive manner.

- Engages in self-evaluation of practice on a regular basis, identifying areas of strength as well as areas in which professional development would be beneficial.

- Obtains informal feedback regarding her or his practice from patients, peers, professional colleagues, and others.

- Participates in peer review as appropriate.

- Takes action to achieve goals identified during the evaluation process.

- Provides the evidence for practice decisions and actions as part of the informal and formal evaluation processes.

- Interacts with peers and colleagues to enhance her or his professional nursing practice or role performance.

- Provides peers with formal or informal constructive feedback regarding their practice or role performance.

ADDITIONAL COMPETENCIES FOR THE GRADUATE-LEVEL PREPARED SPECIALTY NURSE AND THE APRN

The hospice and palliative graduate-level prepared specialty nurse or the advanced practice registered nurse:

- Engages in a formal process seeking feedback regarding her or his practice from patients, peers, professional colleagues, and others.

Standard 15. Resource Utilization

The hospice and palliative registered nurse utilizes appropriate resources to plan and provide nursing services that are safe, effective, and financially responsible.

COMPETENCIES

The hospice and palliative registered nurse:

- Assesses individual patient care needs and resources available to achieve desired outcomes.

- Identifies patient care needs, potential for harm, complexity of the task, and desired outcome when considering resource allocation.

- Delegates elements of care to appropriate healthcare workers in accordance with any applicable legal or policy parameters or principles.

- Identifies the evidence when evaluating resources.

- Advocates for resources, including technology, that enhance nursing practice.

- Modifies practice to promote positive interaction between patients, care providers, and technology as appropriate.

- Assists the patient and family in identifying and securing appropriate and available services to address needs across the healthcare continuum.

- Assists the patient and family in factoring costs, risks, and benefits of treatment and care.

- Participates in the creation of palliative quality measures.

- Determines palliative outcomes and evaluations to establish quality palliative care.

**ADDITIONAL COMPETENCIES FOR THE GRADUATE-LEVEL
PREPARED SPECIALTY NURSE AND THE APRN**

The hospice and palliative graduate-level prepared specialty nurse or the advanced practice registered nurse:

- Utilizes organizational and community resources to formulate inter-professional plans.

- Formulates innovative solutions for patient care problems that utilize resources effectively and maintain quality.

- Designs evaluation strategies that demonstrate cost effectiveness, cost benefit, and efficiency factors associated with nursing practice.

Standard 16. Environmental Health

The hospice and palliative registered nurse practices in an environmentally safe and healthy manner.

COMPETENCIES

The hospice and palliative registered nurse:

- Attains knowledge of environmental health concepts, such as implementation of environmental health strategies.

- Promotes a practice environment that reduces environmental health risks for workers and patients.

- Assesses the practice environment for factors such as sound, odor, noise, and light that threaten health or comfort of patients and staff.

- Advocates for the judicious and appropriate use of resources in health care.

- Communicates environmental health risks and exposure reduction strategies to patients, families, colleagues, and communities.

- Utilizes scientific evidence to determine if a product or treatment is an environmental threat.

- Participates in strategies to promote healthy communities.

ADDITIONAL COMPETENCIES FOR THE GRADUATE-LEVEL PREPARED SPECIALTY NURSE AND THE APRN

The hospice and palliative graduate-level prepared specialty nurse or the advanced practice registered nurse:

- Creates partnerships that promote sustainable environmental health policies and conditions.

- Analyzes the impact of social, political, and economic influences on the environment and human health exposures.

- Critically evaluates the manner in which environmental health issues are presented by the popular media.

- Advocates for implementation of environmental principles for nursing practice.

- Supports nurses in advocating for and implementing environmental principles in nursing practice.

Glossary

Admission process. An activity that begins with the initial referral of an individual to the program of care and continues through the development of the interdisciplinary plan.

Advanced practice registered nurse (APRN). A nurse who has completed an accredited graduate-level education program preparing her or him for the role of certified nurse practitioner, certified registered nurse anesthetist, certified nurse-midwife, or clinical nurse specialist; has passed a national certification examination that measures the APRN role and population-focused competencies; maintains continued competence as evidenced by recertification; and is licensed to practice as an APRN (adapted from APRN Joint Dialogue Group [JDG]; APRN Consensus Work Group & NCSBN APRN Advisory Committee, 2008).

Assessment. A systematic, dynamic process in which the nurse, through interaction with the patient, family, groups, communities, populations, members of the interdisciplinary team, and other healthcare providers, collects and analyzes data. Assessment may include the following dimensions: physical, psychological, sociocultural, spiritual, cognitive, functional abilities, developmental, economic, and lifestyle.

Autonomy. The capacity of a nurse to determine her or his own actions through independent choice, including demonstration of competence, within the full scope of nursing practice (ANA, 2010b).

Caregiver. A person who provides direct care for another, such as a child, dependent adult, the disabled, the progressively seriously ill person, or the person with a terminal illness. In palliative care, especially in hospice, the term *caregiver* can apply to both a family member and paid professional staff.

Code of Ethics (nursing). A set of provisions that makes explicit the primary goals, values, and obligations of the nursing profession and expresses its values, duties, and commitments to the society of which it is a part. In the United States, nurses abide by and adhere to the *Code of Ethics for Nurses* (ANA, 2001).

Collaboration. A professional healthcare partnership grounded in a reciprocal and respectful recognition and acceptance of each partner's unique expertise, power, and sphere of influence and responsibilities; the commonality of goals; the mutual safeguarding of the legitimate interest of each party; and the advantages of such a relationship (ANA, 2010b).

Competency. An expected and measureable level of nursing performance that integrates knowledge, skills, abilities, and judgment, based on established scientific knowledge and expectations for nursing practice (ANA, 2010b).

Consumer. The person, client, family, group, community, or population who is the focus of attention and to whom the registered nurse is providing services as sanctioned by the state regulatory bodies.

Continuing competence. The ongoing commitment of a registered nurse to integrate and apply the knowledge, skills, and judgment with the attitudes, values, and beliefs required to practice safely, effectively, and ethically in a designated role and setting (NBCHPN®, 2011).

Continuity of care. An interdisciplinary process that includes patients, families, and other stakeholders in the development of a coordinated plan. This process facilitates the patient's transition across and between settings and healthcare providers, based on changing needs and available resources.

Delegation. The transfer of responsibility for the performance of a task from one individual to another while retaining accountability for the outcome. Example: The RN, in delegating a task to an assistive individual, transfers the responsibility for performance of the task but retains professional accountability for the overall care.

Diagnosis. A clinical judgment about the patient's response to actual or potential health conditions or needs. The diagnosis provides the basis for development of a plan to achieve expected outcomes. Registered nurses utilize nursing and medical diagnoses depending upon educational and clinical preparation and legal authority. Advanced practice registered nurses utilize medical diagnosis as implied by graduate education, state statutes, and their role as defined by CMS.

Environment. The surrounding context, milieu, conditions, or atmosphere in which a hospice and palliative registered nurse practices.

Environmental health. Aspects of human health, including quality of life, that are determined by physical, chemical, biological, social, and psychological problems in the environment. It also refers to the theory and practice of assessing, correcting, controlling, and preventing those factors in the environment that can potentially adversely affect the health of present and future generations.

Evaluation. The process of determining the progress toward the attainment of expected outcomes, including the effectiveness of care.

Evidence-based practice. A scholarly and systematic problem-solving paradigm that results in the delivery of high-quality health care (ANA, 2010b).

Expected outcomes. End results that are measurable, desirable, and observable, and translate into observable behaviors.

Family. Family of origin or significant others as identified and defined by the patient.

Graduate-level prepared specialty nurse (advanced practice nurse). A registered nurse prepared at the master's or doctoral educational level who has advanced knowledge, skills, abilities, and judgment associated with one or more nursing specialties and is functioning in an advanced level as designated by elements of her or his position. The nurse has completed an accredited graduate-level education program in a nonclinical area such as education or administration.

Health. An experience that is often expressed in terms of wellness and illness, and may occur in the presence or absence of disease or injury.

Healthcare providers. Individuals with special expertise who provide healthcare services or assistance to patients. They may include nurses, physicians, psychologists, social workers, nutritionist/dieticians, pharmacists, nursing assistants, licensed practical/vocational nurses, chaplains, spiritual/bereavement counselors, rehabilitation therapists, and various expressive therapists.

Illness. The subjective experience of discomfort.

Implementation. Activities necessary to enact a plan such as teaching, monitoring, providing, counseling, delegating, and/or coordinating. The patient and family or other members of the interdisciplinary healthcare team may be designated to implement interventions within the plan.

Information. Data that is interpreted, organized, or structured.

Interdisciplinary team. A coordinated group of healthcare professionals who develop a plan to meet the patient's and family's goals. Core members of the hospice interdisciplinary team are the registered nurse and/or advanced practice registered nurse, physician, healthcare or spiritual counselors, and social worker. Other disciplines (e.g., nursing assistant, physical/occupational/speech therapists, dietitian) are brought onto the team based on the patient's and the family's needs. Patients and families are also invited to participate in the team. CMS and NCP define the *palliative care interdisciplinary team* as all the professionals involved in a patient and family's care, including the nurse, the physician, the social worker, the chaplain, rehabilitation specialists, and other expressive therapists as appropriate for the age and development of the patient (NCP, 2013).

Interprofessional. Reliant on the overlapping knowledge, skills, and abilities of each professional team member. This can drive synergistic effects by which outcomes are enhanced and become more comprehensive than a simple aggregation of the individual efforts of the team members.

Medical home or accountable care organizations. Care provision arrangement that uses a primary care model and primary care providers to ensure the delivery of coordinated, comprehensive care.

Nursing. The protection, promotion, and optimization of health and abilities, prevention of illness and injury, alleviation of suffering through the diagnosis and treatment of human response, and advocacy in the care of individuals, families, communities, and populations (ANA, 2010b).

Nursing practice. The collective professional activities of nurses that is characterized by the interrelations of human responses, theory application, nursing actions, and outcomes (ANA, 2010b).

Nursing process. A critical thinking model used by nurses that is comprised by the integration of the singular, concurrent actions of these six components: assessment, diagnosis, identification of outcomes, planning, implementation, and evaluation (ANA, 2010b).

Outcomes (nursing). The results of nursing actions, in relation to identified human responses, based on findings from nursing research, the efficacy and benefit of which are determined by evaluation (ANA, 2010b).

Patient. The person with a diagnosis of a serious or life-threatening illness who is the central focus of palliative care. This person is the one to whom the registered nurse provides services, as sanctioned by state regulatory bodies.

Peer review. A collegial, systematic, and periodic process by which registered nurses are held accountable for practice and which fosters the refinement of one's knowledge, skills, and decision-making at all levels and in all areas of practice.

Plan. A comprehensive outline of the components that are essential to address to attain an expected outcome(s).

Primary palliative nursing. *Nursing* is defined as "the protection, promotion, and optimization of health and abilities, prevention of illness and injury, alleviation of suffering through the diagnosis and treatment of human responses and advocacy in the care of individuals, families, communities, and populations" (ANA, 2010a). Fundamental care of patients with serious or life-threatening illness or injury and their families provided by nonpalliative care specialty registered nurses builds upon their basic nursing education. This allows nurses to provide "patient and family-centered care that optimizes quality of life by anticipating, preventing, and treating suffering" (NCP, 2013, p. 9).

Quality. The degree to which health services for patients, families, groups, communities, or populations increase the likelihood of desired outcomes and are consistent with current professional knowledge. Quality care follows the national quality strategy set forth by the U.S. Department of Health and Human Services in the provisions of the Affordable Care Act (U.S. Department of Health & Human Services, 2012). The strategy includes:

- Making care safer by reducing harm caused in the delivery of care.

- Ensuring that each person and family is engaged as partners in their own care.

- Promoting effective communication and coordination of care.

- Promoting the most effective prevention and treatment practices for the leading causes of mortality, starting with cardiovascular disease.

- Working with communities to promote wide use of best practices to enable healthy living.

- Making quality care more affordable for individuals, families, employers, and governments by developing and spreading new healthcare delivery models (U.S. Department of Health & Human Services, 2012).

Registered nurse (RN). An individual registered or licensed by a state, commonwealth, territory, government, or other regulatory body to practice as a registered nurse (ANA, 2010b).

Scope of nursing practice. The description of the details of nursing practice—specifically, the *who, what, where, when, why,* and *how*—that addresses the range of nursing practice activities common to all registered nurses. When considered in conjunction with the *Standards of Professional Nursing Practice* and the *Code of Ethics for Nurses,* the scope of nursing practice constitutes a comprehensive description of the competent level of nursing common to all registered nurses (ANA, 2010b).

Serious or life-threatening illnesses. A broad range of diagnostic categories in which an individual's daily functioning is adversely affected; stabilization of the condition is unlikely, quality of life is diminished, life expectancy is reduced, and/or the condition and its treatment pose significant burdens. These occur in all populations of patients at all ages (neonates, children, adolescents, and adults) (NCP, 2013, p. 89).

Standards (nursing). Authoritative statements by which the nursing profession describes the responsibilities for which its practitioners are accountable, the outcomes for which registered nurses are responsible, and by which the quality of practice, service, or education can be evaluated (ANA, 2010b).

Standards of Practice. The subset of nursing standards that describes a competent level of nursing care as demonstrated by the nursing process that forms the basis of the decision-making of registered nurses and that encompasses all significant nursing actions (ANA, 2010b). See also *Nursing process*.

Standards of Professional Nursing Practice. The set of nursing standards comprised of the Standards of Practice and the Standards of Professional Performance, with each constituent standard having its own set of key indicators of competence. For a standard to be met, all the listed competencies must be met. When considered in conjunction with the scope of nursing practice, standards comprehensively describe the competent level of nursing common to all registered nurses (ANA, 2010b).

Standards of Professional Performance. The subset of nursing standards that describes a competent level of activities and behavior in the professional role for the registered nurse by which nurses are accountable for their professional actions to themselves, their patients, their peers, and society (ANA, 2010b).

Unit of care. In palliative care, the patient with a chronic serious or life-threatening illness and the patient's family (where family is defined by the patient and broadly includes significant others). The patient and family are an interdependent, integrated whole composed of two or more individuals. They experience individual as well as overlapping needs.

References

American Association of Colleges of Nursing (AACN). (1997). *Peaceful death: Recommended competencies and curricular guidelines for end-of-life.* Washington, DC: Author. Retrieved from www.aacn.nche.edu/Publications/deathfin.htm (accessed June 13, 2013).

American Association of Nurses. (2001). *Code of ethics for nurses with interpretive statements.* Silver Spring, MD: Nursesbooks.org.

American Nurses Association (ANA). (2003). *Position statement: Pain management and control of distressing symptoms in dying patients.*

American Nurses Association (ANA). (2010a). *Nursing: Scope and standards of practice* (2nd ed.). Silver Spring, MD: Nursesbooks.org.

American Nurses Association (ANA). (2010b). *Nursing's social policy statement: The essence of the profession.* Silver Spring, MD: Nursesbooks.org.

American Nurses Association (ANA). (2010c). *Position statement: Registered nurses' roles and responsibilities in providing expert care and counseling at the end of life.* Retrieved from www.nursingworld.org/MainMenuCategories/EthicsStandards/Ethics-Position-Statements/etpain14426.pdf (accessed July 16, 2013).

American Nurses Association (ANA). (2012). *Position statement: Nursing care and do not resuscitate (DNR) and allow natural death (AND) decisions.* Retrieved from www.nursingworld.org/dnrposition (accessed May 29, 2013).

APRN Consensus Work Group & National Council of State Boards of Nursing APRN Advisory Committee. (2008). *Consensus model for APRN regulation: Licensure, accreditation, certification, and education.* Retrieved from www.nursingworld.org/ConsensusModelforAPRN (accessed July 16, 2013).

Bakitas, M., Lyons, K. D., Hegel, M. T., et al. (2009). Effects of a palliative care intervention on clinical outcomes in patients with advanced cancer: The Project ENABLE II randomized controlled trial. *Journal of the American Medical Association, 302*(7), 741–749.

Berry, P. H., Volker, B. G., & Watson, A. C. (2010). An overview of hospice and palliative care. In P. H. Berry (Ed.), *Core curriculum for the generalist hospice and palliative nurse* (3rd ed.) (p. 112). Dubuque, IA: Kendall/Hunt.

Board of Higher Education & Massachusetts Organization of Nurse Executives (BHE/MONE). (2006). *Creativity and connections: Building the framework for the future of nursing education. Report from the Invitational Working Session, March 23–24, 2006.* Burlington, MA: MONE. Retrieved from www.mass.edu/currentinit/documents/ NursingCreativityAndConnections.pdf (accessed July 12, 2013).

Center to Advance Palliative Care. (2013). Growth of palliative care in U.S. Hospitals: 2013 snapshot. Retrieved from www.capc.org/capc-growth-analysis-snapshot-2013.pdf (access October 17, 2013).

Centers for Medicare and Medicaid Services (CMS). (2012). *Title 42: Public health: Part 418—Hospice care.* Retrieved from www.ecfr.gov/cgi-bin/text-idx?c=ecfr&sid=818258235647b14d2961ad30fa3e68e6&rgn=div5&view=te xt&node=42:3.0.1.1.5&idno=42#42:3.0.1.1.5.3.4.12 (accessed July 12, 2013).

Coyle, N. (2010). Introduction to palliative nursing care. In B. R. Ferrell & N. Coyle (Eds.), *Oxford textbook of palliative nursing* (3rd ed.) (p. 311). New York, NY: Oxford University Press.

Dahlin, C. M., & Lynch, M. T. (2013). Evolution of the advanced practice nurse in palliative care. In C. M. Dahlin & M. T. Lynch. (Eds.), *Core curriculum for the advanced practice hospice and palliative registered nurse* (2nd ed.) (p. 112). Pittsburgh, PA: Hospice and Palliative Nurses Association.

Fabrey, L. J., & Chuang, L. (2011). *A national role delineation study of the hospice and palliative registered nurse.* National Board for Certification of Hospice and Palliative Nurses. Retrieved from www.nbchpn.org/DisplayPage. aspx?Title=RN Role Delineation Study (accessed July 16, 2013).

Ferrell, B. R., Virani, R., & Grant, M. (1999). Analysis of end-of-life content in nursing textbooks. *Oncology Nursing Forum, 26*(5), 869–876.

Hospice and Palliative Nurses Association (HPNA). (2002). *Competencies for advanced practice hospice and palliative care nurses.* Dubuque, IA: Kendall/Hunt.

Hospice and Palliative Nurses Association (HPNA). (2004). Position statement: Value of the professional nurse in end-of-life care. *Journal of Hospice and Palliative Nursing, 6*(1), 65–66.

Hospice and Palliative Nurses Association (HPNA). (2007). Position statement: Value of advanced practice nurse in palliative care. *Journal of Hospice and Palliative Nursing, 9*(2), 72–73.

Hospice and Palliative Nurses Association (HPNA). (2010). *Competencies for the generalist hospice and palliative nurse* (2nd ed.). Pittsburgh, PA: Author.

Hospice and Palliative Nurses Association (HPNA). (2011a). *Hospice and Palliative Nurses Association: 2012–2015 research agenda.* Retrieved from www.hpna.org/DisplayPage.aspx?Title=Research (accessed June 21, 2013).

Hospice and Palliative Nurses Association (HPNA). (2011b). *Position statement: The nurse's role in advance care planning.* Retrieved from www.hpna.org/DisplayPage.aspx?Title=Position Statements (accessed June 21, 2013).

Hospice and Palliative Nurses Association (HPNA). (2012). *HPNA position statement: The value of hospice and palliative nursing certification.* Retrieved from www.hpna.org/DisplayPage.aspx?Title=Position Statements (accessed June 21, 2013).

Hospice and Palliative Nurses Association (HPNA). (2013). *Position statement: Assuring high quality palliative care.* Retrieved from www.hpna.org/DisplayPage.aspx?Title=Position Statements (accessed June 21, 2013).

Hospice and Palliative Nurses Association & American Nurses Association. (2007). *Hospice and palliative nursing: Scope and standards of practice* (4th ed.). Silver Spring, MD: nursesbooks.org.

Institute of Medicine (IOM). (1997). *Approaching death: Improving care at the end of life.* Washington, DC: National Academies Press.

Institute of Medicine (IOM). (2010). *The future of nursing: Leading change, advancing health.* Washington, DC: National Academies Press. Retrieved from www.iom.edu/Reports/2010/The-Future-of-Nursing-Leading-Change-Advancing-Health.aspx (accessed July 5, 2013).

The Joint Commission. (2012). *The Joint Commission awards first advanced certifications for palliative care*. Retrieved from www.jointcommission .org/the_joint_commission_awards_first_advanced_certifications_for_ palliative_care/ (accessed July 16, 2013).

Last Acts Task Force. (1997). *Precepts of palliative care*. Task Force on Palliative Care. Retrieved from http://www.aacn.org/WD/Palliative/ Docs/2001Precep.pdf (accessed June 21, 2013).

Lynch, M., Dahlin, C., Hultman, T., & Coakley, E. E. (2011). Palliative care nursing: Defining the discipline? *Journal of Hospice and Palliative Nursing, 13*(2), 106–111.

Mazanec, P. (2011). Self-care strategies. In J. Panke & P. Coyne (Eds.), *Conversations in palliative care* (3rd ed.) (pp. 295–302). Pittsburgh, PA: Hospice and Palliative Nurses Association.

National Board for Certification of Hospice and Palliative Nurses (NBCHPN). (2011). *Statement on continuing competence for nursing: A call to action*. Retrieved from www.nbchpn.org/DisplayPage.aspx?Title=Continuing Competence (accessed June 21, 2013).

National Board for Certification of Hospice and Palliative Nurses (NBCHPN). (2012). *Mission statement*. Retrieved from www.nbchpn.org/DisplayPage .aspx?Title=Mission Statement (accessed June 10, 2013).

National Consensus Project for Quality Palliative Care (NCP). (2013). *Clinical practice guidelines for quality palliative care* (3rd ed.). Pittsburgh, PA: Author.

National Council of State Boards of Nursing APRN Advisory Committee. (2008). *Consensus model for APRN regulation: Licensure, accreditation, certification, and education*. Retrieved from www.ncsbn.org/Consensus_ Model_for_APRN_Regulation_July_2008.pdf (accessed July 12, 2013).

National Hospice and Palliative Care Organization. (2013). *NHPCO's facts and figures: Hospice care in America*. 2013 Edition. Retrieved from www. nhpco.org/sites/default/files/public/Statistics_Research/2013_Facts_ Figures. pdf (accessed October 17, 2013).

National Institute of Nursing Research (NNR). (2011). *Executive summary— The science of compassion: Future directions in end-of-life and palliative care.* Retrieved from www.ninr.nih.gov/NR/rdonlyres/E0A398E2-B881-4958-AE4B-DBDE67472B97/0/EOLPCSummitSummary.pdf (accessed July 14, 2012).

National Quality Forum. (2006). *A national framework and preferred practices for palliative and hospice care quality: A consensus report.* Washington, DC: Author. Retrieved from www.qualityforum.org/Publications/2006/12/A_National_Framework_and_Preferred_Practices_for_Palliative_and_Hospice_Care_Quality.aspx (accessed July 12, 2013).

Promoting Excellence in End-of-Life Care. (2002, July). *A position statement from American nursing leaders.* Missoula, MT: Author. Retrieved from www.promotingexcellence.org/apn/pe3673.html (accessed June 21, 2013).

SUPPORT Principal Investigators. (1995). A controlled trial to improve care for the seriously ill hospitalized patient: The Study to Understand Prognoses and Preferences for Outcomes and Risks of Treatments (SUPPORT). *Journal of the American Medical Association, 274*(20), 1591–1598.

Temel, J. S., Greer, J. A., Muzikansky, A., et al. (2010). Early palliative care for patients with metastatic non-small-cell lung cancer. *New England Journal of Medicine, 363*, 733–742.

U.S. Department of Health & Human Services. (2012). *Annual report to Congress: National strategy for quality improvement in health care.* Retrieved from http://www.ahrq.gov/workingforquality/nqs/nqs2012annlrpt.pdf (accessed July 16, 2013).

Vachon, M. L., & Huggard, J. (2010). Experience of the nurse in end-of-life care in the 21st century: Mentoring the next generation. In B. R. Ferrell & N. Coyle (Eds.), *Oxford textbook of palliative nursing* (3rd ed.) (pp. 1131–1155). New York, NY: Oxford University Press.

Additional Resources

Hospice and Palliative Nurses Association. (2002). *Professional competencies for hospice and palliative nursing assistants.* Dubuque, IA: Kendall/Hunt.

Hospice and Palliative Nurses Association. (2002). *Statement on the scope and standards of hospice and palliative licensed nursing assistant practice.* Dubuque, IA: Kendall/Hunt.

Hospice and Palliative Nurses Association. (2004). *Professional competencies for the hospice and palliative licensed practical/vocational nurse.* Dubuque, IA: Kendall/Hunt.

Hospice and Palliative Nurses Association. (2004). *Statement on the scope and standards of hospice and palliative licensed practical/vocational nursing practice.* Dubuque, IA: Kendall/Hunt.

Hospice and Palliative Nurses Association. (2010). *Position statement: Value of the advanced practice registered nurse in palliative care.* Retrieved from www.hpna.org/DisplayPage.aspx?Title=Position Statements (accessed June 21, 2013).

Hospice and Palliative Nurses Association. (2011). *Position statement: Value of professional nurse in palliative care.* Retrieved from www.hpna.org/DisplayPage.aspx?Title=Position Statements (accessed June 21, 2013).

Hospice Nurses Association. (1995). *Standards of nursing practice and professional performance.* Pittsburgh, PA: Author.

Institute of Medicine. (2001). *Crossing the quality chasm: A new health system for the 21st century.* Washington, DC: National Academies Press.

Institute of Medicine. (2002). *When children die: Improving palliative and end-of-life care for children and their families.* Washington, DC: National Academies Press.

Appendix A.

Hospice and Palliative Nursing: Scope and Standards of Practice (2007)

The content in this appendix is not current and is of historical significance only.

HOSPICE AND PALLIATIVE NURSING:

SCOPE AND STANDARDS

OF PRACTICE

The Publishing Program of ANA

HOSPICE AND PALLIATIVE NURSES ASSOCIATION
AMERICAN NURSES ASSOCIATION
SILVER SPRING, MARYLAND
2007

The content in this appendix is not current and is of historical significance only.

CONTRIBUTORS

Editors

Constance Dahlin, MSN, APRN, BC-PCM
Elaine Glass, MSN, APRN, BC-PCM

Reviewers

Dena Jean Sutermaster, RN, MSN, CHPN®
Judy Lentz, RN, MSN, NHA

ANA Staff

Carol J. Bickford, PhD, RN, BC—Content editor
Yvonne Daley Humes, MSA—Project coordinator
Matthew Seiler, RN, Esq.—Legal counsel

The content in this appendix is not current and is of historical significance only.

CONTENTS

The content in this appendix is not current and is of historical significance only.

The content in this appendix is not current and is of historical significance only.

PREFACE

Statement on the Scope and Standards of Hospice and Palliative Nursing

This document, developed by the Hospice and Palliative Nurses Association, is the fourth edition and represents the cumulative revision of the three previous editions. The first edition, in 1987, focused on basic hospice nursing. The second, in 2000, brought together hospice and palliative care. In 2002, the third edition described the evolution of this specialty nursing practice by addressing both generalist and advanced practice hospice and palliative nursing. This fourth edition is an expansion of the third edition within the American Nurses Association framework.

The hope of the Hospice and Palliative Nurses Association is that these standards will help to further advance the practice of hospice and palliative care and to set benchmarks for all registered nurses and advanced practice nurses who practice nursing within the realm of life-limiting, progressive illness or end-of-life care.

INTRODUCTION

By developing and then articulating the scope and standards of professional nursing practice, the specialty of hospice and palliative nursing informs society about the parameters of nursing practice and guides the formulation of rules and regulations that determine hospice and palliative nursing practice. However, because each state creates its own laws and regulations governing nursing, the designated limits, functions, and titles for nurses, especially those in advanced practice, may vary significantly from state to state. As in all nursing specialties, hospice and palliative nurses must accept professional practice accountability and ensure that their practice remains within the scope of their state nurse practice act, professional code of ethics, and professional practice standards.

Because life-limiting illness increases dramatically with age, hospice and palliative nurses often focus on the care of older adults. The management of these older adults requires special skills.

Nursing practice is differentiated according to the nurse's educational preparation and level of practice. A number of undergraduate programs include coursework in hospice and palliative care. Some graduate nursing programs permit specialization in palliative care; others offer post-master's degree certificates in this area. The hospice and palliative nurse may practice from a generalist through advanced level of competency. In this document, the title Advanced Practice Registered Nurse (APRN) is used as an inclusive term to describe the common core of knowledge, skills, and abilities of both the clinical nurse specialist (CNS) and the nurse practitioner (NP). The advanced practice hospice and palliative nurse demonstrates such advanced competencies to promote the quality of life for individuals and their families experiencing life-limiting, progressive illness. Nursing role specialties include hospice and palliative care case managers and nursing administrators at the executive and manager levels.

The goal of palliative care is to promote the best possible quality of life for patients and families so that they may live as fully and comfortably as possible. Palliative care recognizes dying as part of the normal process of living and focuses on maintaining the quality of remaining life. Palliative care affirms life and neither hastens nor postpones death.

The content in this appendix is not current and is of historical significance only.

Palliative care exists in the hope and belief that through appropriate care and the promotion of a caring community, sensitive to their needs, patients and their families may be free to attain a degree of mental, emotional, and spiritual preparation for death that is satisfactory to them. Although palliative care has no current regulatory time restrictions, hospice care is the final portion of the palliative care continuum regulated by Medicare as a 6-month period if the illness runs its normal course.

Evolution of Hospice and Palliative Nursing

The landmark SUPPORT study (Study to Understand Prognoses and Preferences for Outcomes and Risk of Treatment) by Knaus et al. (1995) highlighted an urgent need for healthcare professionals prepared and committed to improving the quality of life for seriously ill and dying patients and their families. These researchers conducted a two-year prospective observational study with 4,301 patients from teaching hospitals in the United States, followed by a two-year controlled clinical trial with 4,804 patients and their physicians who were randomized either to a control group or to an intervention group that received educational information related to the end of life. Despite the SUPPORT intervention, the study found:

- a continued lack of communication between patients and their physician providers, particularly related to end-of-life preferences,

- an aggressiveness of medical treatments, and

- a high level of pain reported by seriously ill and dying patients.

Knaus et al. believe that improving the experience of seriously ill and dying patients requires an individual and collective commitment of healthcare providers as well as proactive efforts at shaping the caregiving process. Having invested 28 million dollars in the SUPPORT study, the Robert Wood Johnson Foundation (RWJF) has extended its commitment to end-of-life care, recognizing the "overriding need to change the kind of care dying Americans receive" (Last Acts Task Force, 1998).

Educational preparation for end-of-life care has been inconsistent at best and neglected for the most part, in both undergraduate and graduate curricula (AACN, 1997). In accordance with the International Council of Nurses mandate that nurses have a unique and primary responsibility

The content in this appendix is not current and is of historical significance only.

for ensuring the peaceful death of patients, the American Association of Colleges of Nursing (AACN), supported by RWJF, convened a round table of expert nurses to discuss and initiate educational change related to palliative care. These nurse experts concluded that the precepts of hospice care are essential principles for all end-of-life care, and include the following assumptions:

- Persons are living until the moment of death.

- Coordinated care should be offered by a variety of professionals with attention to the physical, psychological, social, and spiritual needs of patients and their families.

- Care should be sensitive to patient and family diversity.

The group proposed that these precepts be added to the foundational content in the education of nurses. The resulting document, "Peaceful Death," outlined baccalaureate competencies for palliative and hospice care and the content areas in which these competencies can be taught (AACN, 1997).

To emphasize the role of nursing in end-of-life care, the American Nurses Association (ANA) issued a position statement regarding the promotion of comfort and relief of pain of dying patients (ANA, 2003). This statement reinforces the nurse's obligation to promote comfort and to ensure aggressive efforts to relieve pain and suffering. Initiatives are underway in nursing to include palliative care content in licensing examinations and to revise nursing textbooks to address palliative care. Specialized palliative care educational initiatives have been offered in the last five years, such as the End-of-life Nursing Education Consortium (ELNEC). ELNEC is supported by a major grant from RWJF to AACN and City of Hope National Medical Center (AACN & CHNMC, 2005).

One goal of undergraduate ELNEC was to train 1,000 nurse educators from associate degree and baccalaureate programs in end-of-life care. Another cohort was to focus on teaching faculty at graduate programs; over 300 graduate program faculty have attended this curriculum. Another program has educated 206 oncology nurses. Pediatric ELNEC faculty members have educated 400 nurses and a new curriculum will focus on end-of-life care in the critical care setting. ELNEC-Geriatrics programs began in February of 2007. The course includes essential content for the highest quality end-of-life geriatric care and is open to long-term-care nurses and hospice nurses who serve patients in long-term care.

The content in this appendix is not current and is of historical significance only.

In 2004, the National Consensus Project (NCP) published *Clinical Practice Guidelines for Quality Palliative Care,* commonly referred to as the *NCP Guidelines.* These guidelines have been endorsed by numerous medical and nursing specialty groups, and encompass populations of all ages. More importantly, the NCP Guidelines served as the foundation of the *National Quality Forum Framework for Preferred Practices for Palliative and Hospice Care,* scheduled to be published in 2007.

National, state, and local indicators point to the need to prepare APRNs who have advanced knowledge and skill in hospice and palliative care, are competent to provide patient care across the life span, and can assume leadership roles in a variety of settings. APRNs can play a vital role in palliative care by assessing, implementing, coordinating, and evaluating care throughout the course of the illness, as well as by counseling and educating patients and families and facilitating continuity of care between hospital and home. Because of their proximity to patients, APRNs are in an ideal position to assess, diagnose, and treat pain and other symptoms. APRNs also identify ethical issues facing individuals and families, develop strategies to assist them in defining expected goals of care, and access and coordinate appropriate care.

Palliative care is a rapidly developing specialty in health care. In September 2006, the American Board of Medical Specialties (ABMS) voted to make hospice and palliative medicine an ABMS subspecialty. Hospice and palliative care services are being developed across the country, including inpatient palliative and hospice units, consultations teams, community or home hospice programs, ambulatory palliative care programs, and programs in skilled nursing facilities. Current estimates are that 30% of hospitals have inpatient palliative care programs (CAPC, 2006).

Professional Association and Certification

In 1987, the Hospice Nurses Association (HNA) was formed. This group became the first professional organization dedicated to promoting excellence in the practice of hospice nursing. Consistent with that goal, the HNA Board of Directors appointed the National Board for the Certification of Hospice Nurses (NBCHN) in 1992. In March of 1994, NBCHN offered the first certification examination and the credential of Certified Registered Nurse Hospice (CRNH).

The content in this appendix is not current and is of historical significance only.

In 1997, recognizing the similarity in the nursing practice of the hospice nurse and the palliative nurse, HNA expanded to embrace palliative nursing practice and became the Hospice and Palliative Nurses Association (HPNA). Hospice and palliative nurses were providing patient and family care in more diverse settings and the fundamental nursing concepts developed in hospices were being applied to other practice environments. The results of the 1998 Role Delineation Study, repeated in 2006, commissioned by NBCHN, revealed only minor differences in practice between end-of-life care offered by hospice nurses and palliative nurses working in non-hospice settings. These differences correlated with requirements of the role or practice setting.

In 1999, NBCHN became the National Board for the Certification of Hospice and Palliative Nurses (NBCHPN®), offering a new professional certification designation to recognize basic competence in hospice and palliative nursing—Certified Hospice and Palliative Nurse (CHPN®), thereby retiring the CRNH credential. In 2004, certification was also offered to APRNs to acknowledge their expertise in palliative care. These were first designated as APRN, BC-PCM. However, with the sole proprietorship of the exam, NBCHPN retired that credential and now APRNs are ACHPNs®. Currently, there are 271 APRNs certified in palliative care.

By 2007, the number of credentialed registered nurses had risen to over 10,000. As demographics change and advanced illnesses and end-of-life needs increase, NBCHPN continues to provide assurance of competency of both generalist and advanced practice registered hospice and palliative nurses who administer care by strengthening the *Scope and Standards of Hospice and Palliative Nursing Practice.*

The content in this appendix is not current and is of historical significance only.

SCOPE OF HOSPICE AND PALLIATIVE NURSING PRACTICE

The scope of practice of hospice and palliative nursing continues to evolve as the science and art of palliative care develops. Hospice and palliative nursing reflects a holistic philosophy of care implemented across the life span and across diverse health settings. In a matrix of affiliation, including the patient and family and other members of the interdisciplinary care team, hospice and palliative nurses provide evidence-based physical, emotional, psychosocial, and spiritual or existential care to individuals and families experiencing life-limiting, progressive illness. The goal of hospice and palliative nursing is to promote and improve the patient's quality of life through the relief of suffering along the course of illness, through the death of the patient, and into the bereavement period of the family. This goal is enhanced by the following activities:

- Comprehensive history: chief complaint, history of present illness, medical and surgical history, family history, social history, immunization history, and allergies

- Review of systems and associated pain and symptoms

- Comprehensive physical and mental status examinations

- Determination of functional status

- Identification of developmental needs for all age groups

- Procurement of appropriate laboratory data and diagnostic studies or procedures

- Determination of effective and ineffective pharmacologic and non-pharmacologic therapies for symptom management

- Identification of past and present goals of care as stated by patient, surrogate, or healthcare proxy or as documented through advanced care planning

- Identification of health beliefs, values, and practices as related to culture, ethnicity, and religion or spirituality

- Recognition of response to advanced illness

- Determination of emotional status such as normal versus complicated grief, depression, anxiety, agitation, and terminal restlessness

The content in this appendix is not current and is of historical significance only.

- Identification of individual–family communication and coping patterns—past and present
- Assessment of patient and family support systems and environmental risks
- Determination of patient and family financial resources
- Assessment of spiritual needs, including meaning of life, illness, and death, as well as a sense of hope or hopelessness, a need for forgiveness, fears, and a connectedness to self, others, nature, and God or a Higher Being

Hospice and palliative care is provided to patients of all ages across the continuum of care from acute care to community care, recognizing that older adults comprise the predominant patient group. Of the 15 leading causes of death, over half are the predominant cause of death in older adults. As with the elderly who are both seriously ill and of limited decision-making capacity, parents or guardians have the responsibility to make the healthcare decisions for their child. This can create significant tensions as the older child is able to become a meaningful participant in care decisions.

Clinical Practice Setting

Practice settings for hospice and palliative nursing are changing in response to the dynamic nature of today's healthcare environment. Hospice and palliative nursing is provided for patients and their families in a variety of care locations including, but not limited to:

- Acute care hospital units
- Long-term-care facilities
- Rehabilitation facilities, assisted living facilities
- Inpatient, home, or residential hospices
- Palliative care clinics or ambulatory settings
- Private practices
- Veterans facilities
- Corrections facilities

The content in this appendix is not current and is of historical significance only.

Levels of Hospice and Palliative Nursing Practice

Hospice and palliative nurses are licensed registered nurses who are educationally prepared in nursing. Hospice and palliative nurses are qualified for specialty practice at two levels: generalist and advanced. These levels are differentiated by education, complexity of practice, and performance of certain nursing functions.

Generalist Level of Hospice and Palliative Nursing Practice

Registered nurses at the generalist level have completed a nursing program and passed the state licensure examination for registered nurses. Registered nurses who practice in hospice and palliative care settings may provide direct patient and family care or function as educators, case managers, nurse clinicians, administrators, and other nursing roles. Their practice should reflect the scope and standards of hospice and palliative nursing delineated in this document.

The generalist competencies in hospice and palliative care, summarized below, represent the knowledge, skills, and abilities demonstrated when providing evidence-based physical, emotional, psychosocial, and spiritual care (HPNA, 2001, 2002). The care is provided in a collaborative manner across the life span in diverse settings to individuals and families experiencing life-limiting, progressive illness.

Clinical Judgment

The hospice and palliative nurse demonstrates critical thinking, analysis, and clinical judgment in all aspects of hospice and palliative care for patients and families experiencing life-limiting illness. This includes use of the nursing process to address the physical, psychosocial, and spiritual needs of patients and families. The generalist and the advanced practice hospice and palliative nurse must respond to all disease processes, including, but not limited to, neurological, cardiac, pulmonary, oncology, renal, hepatic dementias, diabetes, and HIV/AIDS. Clinical judgment is demonstrated in providing effective pain and symptom management.

Advocacy and Ethics

The hospice and palliative nurse incorporates ethical principles and professional standards in the care of patients and families experiencing life-

The content in this appendix is not current and is of historical significance only.

limiting, progressive illnesses. The nurse identifies and advocates for the wishes and preferences of the patient and patient's family, promotes ethical and legal decision making, and improves access to care and community resources by influencing or formulating health and social policy.

Professionalism

The hospice and palliative nurse exhibits knowledge, attitude, behavior, and skills that are consistent with the professional standards, code of ethics, and scope of practice for hospice and palliative nursing. Examples of professionalism include:

- Contributing to improved quality and cost-effective hospice and palliative services.

- Participating in the generation, testing, and evaluation of hospice and palliative care knowledge and practice.

- Participating in the hospice and palliative care organizations.

Collaboration

The hospice and palliative nurse actively promotes dialogue and collaboration with patients and families and facilitates collaborative practice with the healthcare team and community to address and plan for issues related to living with and dying from chronic, life-limiting, progressive illnesses through the bereavement phase.

Systems Thinking

The hospice and palliative nurse identifies and utilizes the system resources necessary to enhance the quality of life for patients and families experiencing life-limiting, progressive illnesses through knowledge and negotiation.

Cultural Competence

The hospice and palliative nurse respects and honors the diversity and unique characteristics of patients, families, and colleagues in hospice and palliative care and bereavement. Cultural competence also means that hospice and palliative nurses address the psychosocial and spiritual needs of patients and families throughout the dying process and bereavement. Cultural values and attitudes are incorporated into the plans of care throughout the continuum.

The content in this appendix is not current and is of historical significance only.

Facilitation of Learning

The hospice and palliative nurse promotes the learning of patient, family, self, members of the healthcare team, and the community by developing, implementing, and evaluating formal and informal education related to living with, and dying from, life-limiting progressive illnesses. This includes creating a healing environment that promotes and permits a peaceful death. The nurse creates opportunities and initiatives for hospice and palliative care education for patients, families, colleagues, and community as well.

Communication

The hospice and palliative nurse uses effective verbal, nonverbal, and written communication with patients and families, members of the healthcare team, and the community at large in order to therapeutically address and accurately convey the hospice and palliative care needs of patients and families throughout the disease process and bereavement. Communication at the generalist level includes using therapeutic communication skills in all interactions throughout the palliative care continuum.

Advanced Practice Level of Hospice and Palliative Nursing Practice

Advanced practice hospice and palliative nursing is an emerging role that responds to the individual, professional, and societal needs related to the experience of life-limiting, progressive illness. The advanced practice hospice and palliative registered nurse is a registered nurse (RN) educated at the master's level or higher in nursing as a clinical nurse specialist (CNS) or nurse practitioner (NP). An advanced practice hospice and palliative registered nurse has the knowledge, skills, and abilities to perform all aspects of basic hospice and palliative nursing as well as to assume the responsibilities of advanced-level care. Advanced practice hospice and palliative registered nurses are distinguished by their ability to synthesize complex data, implement advanced plans of care, and provide leadership in hospice and palliative care. The roles of advanced practice hospice and palliative registered nurses include, but are not limited to:

- Expert clinician
- Leader and facilitator of interdisciplinary teams

The content in this appendix is not current and is of historical significance only.

- Educator

- Researcher

- Consultant

- Collaborator

- Advocate

- Case manager

- Administrator

Advanced practice hospice and palliative nurses who have fulfilled the requirements established by their state nurse practice acts may be authorized to assume autonomous responsibility for clinical role functions, which may include prescription of controlled substances, medications, or therapies. To practice as an advanced practice hospice and palliative registered nurse, national certification in advanced practice hospice and palliative nursing is recommended. The advanced practice hospice and palliative registered nurse may have concurrent advanced practice certification in another specialty as well.

The content in this appendix is not current and is of historical significance only.

STANDARDS OF HOSPICE AND PALLIATIVE NURSING PRACTICE

The standards of hospice and palliative nursing practice are authoritative statements established by the Hospice and Palliative Nurses Association for the nursing profession and the public. The standards identify the responsibilities for which hospice and palliative nurses are accountable. The standards reflect the values and priorities of hospice and palliative nursing and provide a framework for the evaluation of practice. The standards are written in measurable terms and define hospice and palliative nurses' accountability to the public and describe the patient and family outcomes for which they are responsible.

The standards are divided into two sections: the Standards of Practice and the Standards of Professional Performance. Each section identifies criteria that allow the standards to be measured. The criteria include key indicators of competent practice. The standards remain stable over time as they reflect the philosophical values of the profession. However, the criteria should be revised to incorporate advancements in scientific knowledge, technology, and clinical practice. The criteria must be consistent with current nursing practice and reflect evidence-based practice.

Standards of Practice

Standards of practice describe a competent level of generalist and advanced practice registered nursing care, as demonstrated by the nursing process:

- Assessment
- Diagnosis
- Outcomes identification
- Planning
- Implementation (coordination of care, health teaching and health promotion, consultation, and prescriptive authority and treatment)
- Evaluation

The content in this appendix is not current and is of historical significance only.

STANDARDS OF PRACTICE

The development and maintenance of a therapeutic nurse–patient and family relationship is essential throughout the nursing process. The nursing process forms the foundation of clinical decision making and encompasses all significant actions taken by hospice and palliative nurses in providing care to individuals and families. Several recurrent themes of nursing practice require attention:

- Providing age-appropriate, culturally, ethnically, and spiritually sensitive care and support

- Maintaining a safe environment

- Educating patients and families to identify appropriate settings and treatment options

- Assuring continuity of care and transitioning to the next appropriate setting

- Coordinating care across settings and among caregivers

- Managing information and protecting confidentiality

- Communicating promptly and effectively

A fundamental practice focus for hospice and palliative care is the plan of care, which is developed with the patient and family (with them as the center of care) and the interdisciplinary team in all practice activities. At the very minimum, the interdisciplinary team must include the physician, the nurse, the social worker, and clergy. Care responsibilities extend beyond the death of the patient to include a minimum of at least a year for bereavement care.

In addition to the distinct levels of nursing care—generalist and advanced—hospice and palliative nurses fulfill other roles. The nursing role specialty most prominent in hospice and palliative nursing is the hospice and palliative case manager. The case manager facilitates the activities of the interdisciplinary team within the regulatory requirements published as the Conditions of Participation as defined by the Health and Human Services Department. Specific criteria are included in this document to address the standards of practice of this role.

The content in this appendix is not current and is of historical significance only.

Standards of Professional Performance

Standards of professional performance and the associated measurement criteria describe competent professional role behaviors, including activities related to:

- Quality of practice
- Education
- Professional practice evaluation
- Collegiality
- Collaboration
- Ethics
- Research
- Resource utilization
- Leadership

Hospice and palliative nurses must be self-directed and purposeful in seeking necessary knowledge and skills to develop and maintain their competency. Hospice and palliative nurses' professionalism is enhanced through membership in their professional organizations, certification in their specialty, and professional development through academic and continuing education.

The content in this appendix is not current and is of historical significance only.

STANDARDS OF HOSPICE AND PALLIATIVE NURSING PRACTICE
STANDARDS OF PRACTICE

STANDARD 1. ASSESSMENT
The hospice and palliative registered nurse collects comprehensive data pertinent to the patient's health or the situation.

Measurement Criteria:

The hospice and palliative registered nurse:

- Collects data in a systematic and ongoing process using critical thinking, analysis, and judgment.

- Involves the patient, family, other healthcare providers, and environment, as appropriate, in holistic data collection.

- Prioritizes data collection activities based on the patient's immediate condition or anticipated needs of the patient, the family, or the situation.

- Adapts assessment techniques to address the differing physiological and psychosocial characteristics of older and younger patients.

- Uses appropriate evidence-based assessment and research techniques and instruments in collecting pertinent data.

- Uses analytical models and problem-solving tools.

- Synthesizes available data, information, and knowledge relevant to the situation to identify patterns and variances.

- Documents relevant data in an organized and retrievable format.

- Communicates to other interdisciplinary team members and consultants.

Continued ▶

The content in this appendix is not current and is of historical significance only.

Additional Measurement Criteria for the Advanced Practice Hospice and Palliative Registered Nurse:

The advanced practice hospice and palliative registered nurse:

- Prescribes and interprets diagnostic tests and procedures relevant to the patient's current status.

- Organizes family meetings to determine the patient's and family members' wishes and preferences and to identify areas of conflict, agreement, and understanding among each other and with the healthcare team.

- Reviews allergies and current medications for maximum effectiveness and possible need for adjustment based on further assessments.

The content in this appendix is not current and is of historical significance only.

STANDARD 2. DIAGNOSIS
The hospice and palliative registered nurse analyzes the assessment data to determine nursing diagnoses or issues.

Measurement Criteria:

The hospice and palliative registered nurse:

- Derives the nursing diagnoses or issues based on assessment data, which includes actual or potential responses to alterations in health.

- Validates the nursing diagnoses or issues with the patient, the family, and the interdisciplinary team as well as other healthcare providers when possible and appropriate.

- Recognizes the influence of age on the patient's condition when formulating nursing diagnoses.

- Documents nursing diagnoses or issues in a manner that facilitates the determination of the expected outcomes and plan of care.

- Communicates to other interdisciplinary team members or consultants.

Additional Measurement Criteria for the Advanced Practice Hospice and Palliative Registered Nurse:

The advanced practice hospice and palliative registered nurse:

- Systematically compares and contrasts clinical findings with normal and abnormal variations and developmental events in formulating a differential diagnosis.

- Utilizes complex data and information obtained during interview, examination, diagnostic procedures, and family meetings in identifying nursing diagnoses.

- Assists staff in developing and maintaining competency in the diagnostic process.

The content in this appendix is not current and is of historical significance only.

STANDARD 3. OUTCOMES IDENTIFICATION
The hospice and palliative registered nurse, in partnership with the interdisciplinary healthcare team, identifies expected outcomes for a plan of care individualized to the patient or the situation.

Measurement Criteria:

The hospice and palliative registered nurse:

- Involves the patient, family, interdisciplinary team, and other healthcare providers in formulating expected outcomes to improve quality of life.

- Derives age- and culturally appropriate expected outcomes from the nursing diagnoses.

- Considers associated risks, benefits, costs, current scientific evidence, and clinical expertise when formulating expected outcomes.

- Defines expected outcomes in terms of the patient's and family's goals of care, the patient's values, ethical considerations, environment, or situation, with such consideration as associated risks, benefits and costs, and current scientific evidence.

- Includes a time estimate for attainment of expected outcomes.

- Develops expected outcomes that provide direction for continuity of care across care settings and through the family bereavement.

- Modifies expected outcomes based on changes in the status of the patient or evaluation of the situation.

- Documents expected outcomes as measurable goals.

- Communicates to other interdisciplinary team members and consultants.

Additional Measurement Criteria for the Advanced Practice Hospice and Palliative Registered Nurse:

The advanced practice hospice and palliative registered nurse:

- Identifies expected outcomes that incorporate scientific evidence and are achievable through implementation of evidence-based practices.

- Conducts family meetings periodically to clarify and reaffirm the goals of care.

The content in this appendix is not current and is of historical significance only.

- Identifies expected outcomes that incorporate both cost and clinical effectiveness, patient satisfaction, and continuity and consistency among providers.

- Supports the use of clinical guidelines linked to positive patient outcomes.

- Utilizes the knowledge that expected outcomes in older adults often differ from outcomes among younger individuals and pediatric patients.

The content in this appendix is not current and is of historical significance only.

STANDARD 4. PLANNING
The hospice and palliative registered nurse develops a plan of care that prescribes strategies and alternatives to attain expected outcomes.

Measurement Criteria:

The hospice and palliative registered nurse:

- Promotes the patient's power of choice in decision making.

- Develops an individualized plan of care that considers patient characteristics or the situation (e.g., age- and culturally appropriate, environmentally sensitive).

- Develops the plan of care negotiated in conjunction with the patient, family, interdisciplinary team, and others, as appropriate.

- Includes strategies within the plan of care that address each of the identified nursing diagnoses or issues, which may include strategies for promotion and restoration of health and prevention of illness, injury, and disease.

- Provides for continuity within the plan of care across settings and through the family bereavement.

- Incorporates an implementation pathway or timeline within the plan of care.

- Establishes priorities within the plan of care with the patient, family, interdisciplinary team, and others as appropriate.

- Utilizes the plan of care to provide direction and regular updates to other members of the healthcare team.

- Defines the plan of care to reflect current statutes, rules and regulations, and standards.

- Integrates current best practices and research affecting care in the planning process.

- Considers the economic impact of the plan of care.

- Uses standardized language or recognized terminology to document the plan of care.

- Communicates to other interdisciplinary team members and consultants.

The content in this appendix is not current and is of historical significance only.

Additional Measurement Criteria for the Advanced Practice Hospice and Palliative Registered Nurse:

The advanced practice hospice and palliative registered nurse:

- Identifies assessment, diagnostic strategies, and therapeutic interventions within the plan of care that reflect current evidence, including data, research, literature, expert clinical knowledge, and collaboration from others when necessary.

- Selects or designs strategies to meet the multifaceted needs of complex patients, and physiological and psychosocial changes common to all ages, including consulting with other experts in developing the plan of care.

- Includes the synthesis of patient and family values and beliefs regarding nursing and medical therapies within the plan of care.

Additional Measurement Criteria for the Hospice and Palliative Registered Nurse in a Nursing Role Specialty:

The hospice and palliative registered nurse in a nursing role specialty:

- Participates in the design and development of multidisciplinary and interdisciplinary processes to address the typical life-limiting, progressive illness.

- Contributes to the development and continuous improvement of organizational systems that support the planning process.

- Supports the integration of clinical, human, and financial resources to enhance and complete the critical thinking needed in planning processes.

The content in this appendix is not current and is of historical significance only.

STANDARD 5. IMPLEMENTATION
The hospice and palliative registered nurse implements the identified plan of care.

Measurement Criteria:

The hospice and palliative registered nurse:

- Implements the plan of care in a safe, timely, and culturally competent manner.

- Documents implementation and any modifications, including changes or omissions, of the identified plan of care.

- Utilizes evidence-based interventions and treatments specific to the diagnoses or problems.

- Collaborates with patient, family members, nursing colleagues, interdisciplinary team, and others to implement the plan of care.

- Utilizes community resources and systems to implement the plan of care.

- Promotes quality of life for individuals and families by relieving suffering.

- Advocates to promote self-determination, resolve conflicts, and ensure ethically appropriate care.

Additional Measurement Criteria for the Advanced Practice Hospice and Palliative Registered Nurse:

The advanced practice hospice and palliative registered nurse:

- Facilitates identification and utilization of systems and community resources to implement the plan.

- Collaborates with patients, family members, nursing colleagues, the palliative care interdisciplinary team, and other appropriate healthcare providers to implement the plan.

- Incorporates new knowledge and strategies to initiate change in nursing care practices if desired outcomes are not achieved.

The content in this appendix is not current and is of historical significance only.

Additional Measurement Criteria for the Hospice and Palliative Registered Nurse in a Nursing Role Specialty:

The hospice and palliative registered nurse in a nursing role specialty:

- Implements the plan using principles and concepts of project or systems management.

- Fosters organizational systems that support implementation of the plan of care.

The content in this appendix is not current and is of historical significance only.

STANDARD 5A: COORDINATION OF CARE
The hospice and palliative registered nurse coordinates care delivery.

Measurement Criteria:

The hospice and palliative registered nurse:

- Coordinates implementation of the plan of care.

- Documents the coordination of interdisciplinary care.

- Considers the complexity of coordination of care for patients of all ages, their families, and caregivers.

Measurement Criteria for the Advanced Practice Hospice and Palliative Registered Nurse:

The advanced practice hospice and palliative registered nurse:

- Provides leadership in the coordination of interdisciplinary health care for integrated delivery of patient care services.

- Synthesizes data and information to prescribe necessary medications, treatments, consultations, and system and community support measures, including environmental modifications.

- Coordinates system and community resources that enhance delivery of care across the healthcare continuum.

The content in this appendix is not current and is of historical significance only.

STANDARD 5B: HEALTH TEACHING AND HEALTH PROMOTION
The hospice and palliative registered nurse employs strategies to promote health and a safe environment.

Measurement Criteria:

The hospice and palliative registered nurse:

- Provides health teaching that addresses such topics as healthy lifestyles, risk-reducing behaviors, developmental needs, activities of daily living, and preventive self-care.

- Uses health promotion and health teaching methods appropriate to the situation and the patient's developmental level, learning needs, readiness, ability to learn, language preference, spiritual preference, and culture.

- Seeks opportunities for feedback and evaluation of the effectiveness of the strategies used.

Additional Measurement Criteria for the Advanced Practice Hospice and Palliative Registered Nurse:

The advanced practice hospice and palliative registered nurse:

- Synthesizes empirical evidence on risk behaviors, learning theories, behavioral change theories, motivational theories, epidemiology, and other related theories and frameworks when designing health information and patient and family education.

- Designs health information and education for the patient and family appropriate to their developmental level, learning needs, readiness to learn, and cultural values and beliefs.

- Utilizes geriatric best practices as a basis for health promotion, maintenance, and teaching related to older adults, their families, and caregivers.

- Evaluates health information resources, including the Internet, within the area of practice for accuracy, readability, and comprehensibility to help patients access quality health information.

The content in this appendix is not current and is of historical significance only.

Standard 5c: Consultation

The advanced practice hospice and palliative registered nurse and the nursing role specialist provide consultation to influence the identified plan, enhance the abilities of others, and effect change.

Measurement Criteria for the Advanced Practice Hospice and Palliative Registered Nurse:

The advanced hospice and palliative practice registered nurse:

- Synthesizes clinical data, theoretical frameworks, and evidence when providing consultation.

- Facilitates the effectiveness of a consultation by involving the patient and family in decision making and negotiating role responsibilities.

- Communicates consultation recommendations that facilitate change for the patient, family, and all caregivers.

Measurement Criteria for the Hospice and Palliative Registered Nurse in a Nursing Role Specialty:

The hospice and palliative registered nurse in a nursing role specialty:

- Synthesizes data, information, theoretical frameworks, and evidence when providing consultation.

- Facilitates the effectiveness of a consultation by involving the stakeholders in the decision-making process.

- Communicates consultation recommendations that influence the identified plan.

- Facilitates understanding by involved stakeholders, enhancing the work of others, and effecting change.

The content in this appendix is not current and is of historical significance only.

STANDARD 5D: PRESCRIPTIVE AUTHORITY AND TREATMENT

The advanced practice hospice and palliative registered nurse uses prescriptive authority, procedures, referrals, treatments, and therapies in accordance with state and federal laws and regulations.

Measurement Criteria for the Advanced Practice Hospice and Palliative Registered Nurse:

The advanced practice hospice and palliative registered nurse:

- Prescribes evidence-based treatments, therapies, and procedures considering the patient's comprehensive healthcare needs.

- Prescribes pharmacologic agents based on a current knowledge of pharmacology, physiology and physiologic changes, pharmacodynamic, and medication adherence common to older adults.

- Prescribes specific pharmacological agents and treatments based on clinical indicators, the patient's status and needs, and the results of diagnostic and laboratory tests.

- Orders referral or consults to other disciplines to meet the patient's needs (e.g., physical therapy, behavioral medicine, massage therapy, healing touch).

- Evaluates therapeutic and potential adverse effects of pharmacological and non-pharmacological treatments.

- Provides patients with information about intended effects and potential adverse effects of proposed prescriptive therapies.

- Provides information about financial considerations of evidence-based therapies, and alternative treatments and procedures, as appropriate.

The content in this appendix is not current and is of historical significance only.

STANDARD 6. EVALUATION
The hospice and palliative registered nurse evaluates progress towards attainment of outcomes.

Measurement Criteria:

The hospice and palliative registered nurse:

- Conducts a systematic, ongoing, and criterion-based evaluation of the outcomes in relation to the structures and processes prescribed by the plan of care and the indicated timeline.

- Includes the patient, family, and others involved in the care or situation in the evaluative process.

- Evaluates the effectiveness of the planned strategies in relation to patient responses and the attainment of the expected outcomes.

- Documents the results of the evaluation.

- Uses ongoing assessment data to revise the nursing diagnoses, outcomes, the plan of care, and the implementation as needed.

- Disseminates the evaluation results to the patient, family, interdisciplinary team, and others involved in the care or situation, as appropriate, in accordance with state and federal laws and regulations.

Additional Measurement Criteria for the Advanced Practice Hospice and Palliative Registered Nurse:

The advanced practice hospice and palliative registered nurse:

- Evaluates the accuracy of the diagnosis and effectiveness of the interventions in relationship to the patient's attainment of expected outcomes.

- Synthesizes the results of the evaluation analyses to determine the impact of the plan of care on the affected patients, families, groups, communities, and institutions.

- Uses the results of the evaluation analyses to make or recommend process or structural changes including policy, procedure, or protocol documentation, as appropriate.

The content in this appendix is not current and is of historical significance only.

Additional Measurement Criteria for the Hospice and Palliative Registered Nurse in a Nursing Role Specialty:

The hospice and palliative registered nurse in a nursing role specialty:

- Uses the results of the evaluation analyses to make or recommend process or structural changes including policy, procedure, or protocol documentation, as appropriate.

- Synthesizes the results of the evaluation analyses to determine the impact of the plan on the affected patients, families, groups, communities, institutions, networks, and organizations.

The content in this appendix is not current and is of historical significance only.

STANDARDS OF PROFESSIONAL PERFORMANCE

STANDARD 7. QUALITY OF PRACTICE
The hospice and palliative registered nurse systematically enhances the quality and effectiveness of nursing practice.

Measurement Criteria:

The hospice and palliative registered nurse:

- Demonstrates quality by documenting the application of the nursing process in a responsible, accountable, and ethical manner.

- Uses the results of quality improvement activities to initiate changes in nursing practice and in the healthcare delivery system.

- Uses creativity and innovation in nursing practice to improve care delivery.

- Incorporates new knowledge to initiate changes in nursing practice if desired outcomes are not achieved.

- Participates in quality improvement activities. Such activities may include:

  - Identifying aspects of practice important for quality monitoring.

  - Using indicators developed to monitor quality and effectiveness of nursing practice.

  - Collecting data to monitor quality and effectiveness of nursing practice.

  - Analyzing quality data to identify opportunities for improving nursing practice.

  - Formulating recommendations to improve nursing practice or outcomes.

  - Implementing activities to enhance the quality of nursing practice.

  - Developing, implementing, and evaluating policies, procedures, and guidelines to improve the quality of practice.

Continued ▶

The content in this appendix is not current and is of historical significance only.

- Participating on interdisciplinary teams to evaluate clinical care or health services.

- Participating in efforts to minimize costs and unnecessary duplication.

- Analyzing factors related to safety, satisfaction, effectiveness, and cost–benefit options.

- Analyzing organizational systems for barriers.

- Implementing processes to remove or decrease barriers within organizational systems.

Additional Measurement Criteria for the Advanced Practice Hospice and Palliative Registered Nurse:

The advanced practice hospice and palliative registered nurse:

- Obtains and maintains professional certification in the area of expertise.

- Designs quality improvement initiatives.

- Implements initiatives to evaluate the need for change within organizational systems.

- Evaluates the practice environment and quality of nursing care rendered in relation to existing evidence, identifying opportunities for the generation and use of research.

- Bases evaluation on current knowledge, practice, and research common to older adults.

- Participates in research activities.

Additional Measurement Criteria for the Hospice and Palliative Registered Nurse in a Nursing Role Specialty:

The hospice and palliative registered nurse in a nursing role specialty:

- Obtains and maintains professional certification if available in the area of expertise.

- Designs quality improvement initiatives.

- Implements initiatives to evaluate the need for change.

- Evaluates the practice environment in relation to existing evidence, identifying opportunities for the generation and use of research.

The content in this appendix is not current and is of historical significance only.

STANDARD 8. EDUCATION
The hospice and palliative registered nurse attains knowledge and competency that reflects current hospice and palliative nursing practice.

Measurement Criteria:

The hospice and palliative registered nurse:

- Participates in ongoing educational activities related to appropriate knowledge bases and professional issues.

- Demonstrates a commitment to lifelong learning through self-reflection and inquiry to identify learning needs.

- Seeks experiences that reflect current practice in order to maintain skills and competence in clinical practice or role performance.

- Acquires knowledge and skills appropriate to the specialty area, practice setting, role, or situation.

- Maintains professional records that provide evidence of competency and lifelong learning.

- Seeks experiences and formal and independent learning activities to maintain and develop clinical and professional skills and knowledge.

Additional Measurement Criteria for the Advanced Practice Hospice and Palliative Registered Nurse:

The advanced practice hospice and palliative registered nurse:

- Uses current healthcare research findings and other evidence to expand clinical knowledge, enhance role performance, and increase knowledge of professional issues.

- Provides inservice education to others in the area of interest.

- Provides presentations to local, state, national, and international conferences in area of expertise.

- Offers to precept nursing and other professional students.

- Educates advocates, lobbyists, and politicians as needed on nursing and healthcare issues.

Continued ▶

The content in this appendix is not current and is of historical significance only.

Additional Measurement Criteria for the Hospice and Palliative Registered Nurse in a Nursing Role Specialty:

The hospice and palliative registered nurse in a nursing role specialty:

- Uses current research findings and other evidence to expand knowledge, enhance role performance, and increase knowledge of professional issues.

- Precepts nursing students, new employees, and ancillary staff.

The content in this appendix is not current and is of historical significance only.

STANDARD 9. PROFESSIONAL PRACTICE EVALUATION
The hospice and palliative registered nurse evaluates one's own nursing practice in relation to professional practice standards and guidelines, relevant statutes, rules, and regulations.

Measurement Criteria:

The hospice and palliative registered nurse's practice reflects the application of knowledge of current practice standards, guidelines, statutes, rules, and regulations.

The hospice and palliative registered nurse:

- Provides age-appropriate care in a culturally and ethnically sensitive manner.

- Engages in self-evaluation of practice on a regular basis, identifying areas of strength as well as areas in which professional development would be beneficial.

- Obtains informal feedback regarding one's own practice from patients, peers, professional colleagues, and others.

- Participates in systematic peer review as appropriate.

- Takes action to achieve goals identified during the evaluation process.

- Provides rationales for practice beliefs, decisions, and actions as part of the informal and formal evaluation processes.

Additional Measurement Criteria for the Advanced Practice Hospice and Palliative Registered Nurse:

The advanced practice hospice and palliative registered nurse:

- Engages in a peer review formal process seeking feedback regarding one's own practice from patients, peers, professional colleagues, and others.

- Provides constructive and sensitive feedback to others regarding their practice with a focus on improvement of nursing practice and achievement of excellence.

Continued ▶

The content in this appendix is not current and is of historical significance only.

Additional Measurement Criteria for the Hospice and Palliative Registered Nurse in a Nursing Role Specialty:

The hospice and palliative registered nurse in a nursing role specialty:

- Engages in a formal process seeking feedback regarding role performance from individuals, professional colleagues, representatives and administrators of corporate entities, and others.

The content in this appendix is not current and is of historical significance only.

STANDARD 10. COLLEGIALITY

The hospice and palliative registered nurse interacts with and contributes to the professional development of peers and colleagues.

Measurement Criteria:

The hospice and palliative registered nurse:

- Shares knowledge and skills with peers and colleagues as evidenced by such activities as patient care conferences or presentations at formal or informal meetings.

- Provides peers with feedback regarding their practice and role performance.

- Interacts with peers and colleagues to enhance one's own professional nursing practice and role performance.

- Maintains compassionate and caring relationships with peers and colleagues.

- Contributes to an environment that is conducive to the education of healthcare professionals.

- Contributes to a supportive and healthy work environment.

Additional Measurement Criteria for the Advanced Practice Hospice and Palliative Registered Nurse:

The advanced practice hospice and palliative registered nurse:

- Models expert practice to interdisciplinary team members and healthcare consumers.

- Mentors other registered nurses and colleagues as appropriate.

- Participates with interdisciplinary teams that contribute to role development and advanced nursing practice and health care.

- Assesses the emotional climate of the work environment and takes appropriate actions to improve the situation.

- Assesses the emotional, spiritual, and social needs of others on the interdisciplinary team and takes appropriate action to assist those in distress.

Continued ▶

The content in this appendix is not current and is of historical significance only.

STANDARDS OF PROFESSIONAL PERFORMANCE

Additional Measurement Criteria for the Hospice and Palliative Registered Nurse in a Nursing Role Specialty:

The hospice and palliative registered nurse in a nursing role specialty:

- Participates on interdisciplinary and multi-professional teams that contribute to role development and, directly or indirectly, advance nursing practice and health services.

- Mentors other hospice and palliative registered nurses and colleagues as appropriate.

- Assists new interdisciplinary team members to become part of the team.

The content in this appendix is not current and is of historical significance only.

STANDARD 11. COLLABORATION

The hospice and palliative registered nurse collaborates with the patient, the family, the interdisciplinary team, and others in the conduct of nursing practice.

Measurement Criteria:

The hospice and palliative registered nurse:

- Communicates with the patient, the family, the interdisciplinary team, and healthcare providers regarding patient care and the nurse's role in the provision of that care.

- Collaborates in creating a documented plan focused on outcomes and decisions related to care and delivery of services that indicates communication with patients, families, and others.

- Partners with others to effect change and generate positive outcomes through knowledge of the patient, family, or situation.

- Documents referrals, including provisions for continuity of care.

Additional Measurement Criteria for the Advanced Practice Hospice and Palliative Registered Nurse:

The advanced practice hospice and palliative registered nurse:

- Partners with other disciplines to enhance patient care through interdisciplinary activities such as education, consultation, management, technological development, or research opportunities.

- Facilitates an interdisciplinary process with other members of the healthcare team.

- Documents plan-of-care communications, rationales for plan-of-care changes, and collaborative discussions to improve patient care.

Continued ▶

The content in this appendix is not current and is of historical significance only.

STANDARDS OF PROFESSIONAL PERFORMANCE

Additional Measurement Criteria for the Hospice and Palliative Registered Nurse in a Nursing Role Specialty:

The hospice and palliative registered nurse in a nursing role specialty:

- Partners with others to enhance health care and ultimately patient care, through interdisciplinary activities such as education, consultation, management, technological development, or research opportunities.

- Participates in the revision process of local, state, and federal regulations when possible.

- Documents plans, communications, rationales for plan-of-care changes and collaborative discussions with consideration of regulatory and governmental constraints.

The content in this appendix is not current and is of historical significance only.

STANDARD 12. ETHICS
The hospice and palliative registered nurse integrates ethical provisions in all areas of practice.

Measurement Criteria:

The hospice and palliative registered nurse:

- Uses *Code of Ethics for Nurses with Interpretive Statements* (ANA, 2001) to guide practice.

- Delivers care in a manner that preserves and protects patient autonomy, cultural preferences, dignity, and rights, and honors the patient's wishes.

- Maintains patient confidentiality within legal and regulatory parameters.

- Actively participates in the informed consent process (including the right to choose) for patients' procedures, tests, treatments, and research participation, as appropriate, by educating, advocating, and clarifying options to the patient and family.

- Serves as a patient advocate, assisting patients in developing skills for self advocacy.

- Maintains a therapeutic and professional patient–nurse relationship within appropriate professional role boundaries.

- Demonstrates a commitment to practicing self-care, managing stress, and connecting with self and others.

- Contributes to resolving ethical issues of patients, colleagues, or systems as evidenced in such activities as requesting an ethics consult in a confidential, non-punitive manner.

- Reports illegal, incompetent, or impaired practices.

Continued ▶

The content in this appendix is not current and is of historical significance only.

STANDARDS OF PROFESSIONAL PERFORMANCE

Additional Measurement Criteria for the Advanced Practice Hospice and Palliative Registered Nurse:

The advanced practice hospice and palliative registered nurse:

- Informs the patient of the risks, benefits, and outcomes of health-care regimens.

- Participates in interdisciplinary teams that address ethical risks, benefits, and outcomes of practice.

- Articulates a working knowledge of end-of-life ethical issues, including state law regarding Do Not Resuscitate, research pros and cons of artificial nutrition, state law on ethical concerns regarding withdrawal of life support, etc.

Additional Measurement Criteria for the Hospice and Palliative Registered Nurse in a Nursing Role Specialty:

The hospice and palliative registered nurse in a nursing role specialty:

- Participates on multidisciplinary and interdisciplinary teams that address ethical risks, benefits, and outcomes.

- Informs administrators or others of the risks, benefits, and outcomes of programs and decisions that affect healthcare delivery.

The content in this appendix is not current and is of historical significance only.

STANDARD 13. RESEARCH
The hospice and palliative registered nurse integrates research findings into practice.

Measurement Criteria:

The hospice and palliative registered nurse:

- Utilizes the best available evidence, including research findings, to guide practice decisions.

- Actively participates in research activities at various levels appropriate to the nurse's level of education and position. Such activities may include:

  - Identifying clinical problems specific to nursing research (patient care and nursing practice).

  - Participating in data collection (surveys, pilot projects, formal studies).

  - Participating in a formal committee or program.

  - Sharing research activities and findings with peers and others.

  - Conducting research.

  - Critically analyzing and interpreting research for application to practice.

  - Using research findings in the development of policies, procedures, and standards of practice in patient care.

  - Incorporating research as a basis for learning methods to improve patient care.

Additional Measurement Criteria for the Advanced Practice Hospice and Palliative Registered Nurse:

The advanced practice hospice and palliative registered nurse:

- Contributes to nursing knowledge by conducting or synthesizing research that discovers, examines, and evaluates knowledge, theories, criteria, and creative approaches to improve healthcare practice.

- Formally disseminates research findings through activities such as presentations, publications, consultation, and journal clubs.

Continued ▶

Standards of Professional Performance

Additional Measurement Criteria for the Hospice and Palliative Registered Nurse in a Nursing Role Specialty:

The hospice and palliative registered nurse in a nursing role specialty:

- Contributes to nursing knowledge by conducting or synthesizing research that discovers, examines, and evaluates knowledge, theories, criteria, and creative approaches to improve health care within the required regulations.

- Formally disseminates research findings through activities such as presentations, publications, consultation, and journal clubs.

The content in this appendix is not current and is of historical significance only.

STANDARD 14. RESOURCE UTILIZATION
The hospice and palliative registered nurse considers factors related to safety, effectiveness, cost, and impact on practice in the planning and delivery of nursing services.

Measurement Criteria:

The hospice and palliative registered nurse:

- Evaluates factors such as safety, effectiveness, availability, cost and benefits, efficiencies, and impact on practice, when choosing practice options that would result in the same expected outcome.

- Assists the patient and family in identifying and securing appropriate and available services to address health-related needs.

- Assigns or delegates tasks, based on the needs and condition of the patient, potential for harm, stability of the patient's condition, complexity of the task, and predictability of the outcome.

- Assists the patient and family in becoming informed consumers about the options, costs, risks, and benefits of treatment and care.

Additional Measurement Criteria for the Advanced Practice Hospice and Palliative Registered Nurse:

The advanced practice hospice and palliative registered nurse:

- Utilizes organizational and community resources to formulate multidisciplinary or interdisciplinary plans of care.

- Develops innovative solutions for patient care problems that address effective resource utilization and maintenance of quality.

- Develops evaluation strategies to demonstrate cost effectiveness, cost benefit, and efficiency factors associated with nursing practice.

Continued ▶

The content in this appendix is not current and is of historical significance only.

STANDARDS OF PROFESSIONAL PERFORMANCE

Additional Measurement Criteria for the Hospice and Palliative Registered Nurse in a Nursing Role Specialty:

The hospice and palliative registered nurse in a nursing role specialty:

- Develops innovative solutions and applies strategies to obtain appropriate resources for nursing initiatives.

- Secures organizational resources to ensure a work environment conducive to completing the identified plan and outcomes.

- Develops evaluation methods to measure safety and effectiveness for interventions and outcomes.

- Promotes activities that assist others, as appropriate, in becoming informed about costs, risks, and benefits of care or of the plan and solution.

The content in this appendix is not current and is of historical significance only.

STANDARD 15. LEADERSHIP
The hospice and palliative registered nurse provides leadership in the professional practice setting and the profession.

Measurement Criteria:

The hospice and palliative registered nurse:

- Engages in teamwork as a team player, a team builder, and a team leader.

- Works to create and maintain healthy work environments.

- Displays the ability to define a clear vision of associated goals and to plan, implement, and measure progress.

- Demonstrates a commitment to continuous, lifelong learning for self and others.

- Facilitates teaching others to succeed by mentoring and other strategies.

- Exhibits creativity and flexibility through times of change.

- Demonstrates energy, excitement, joy, and a passion for quality work.

- Willingly accepts mistakes by self and others, thereby creating a culture in which risk-taking is not only safe but expected.

- Inspires loyalty through valuing of people as the most precious asset in an organization.

- Directs the coordination of care across settings and among caregivers, including oversight of licensed and unlicensed personnel in any assigned or delegated tasks.

- Serves in key roles in the work setting by participating on committees, councils, and administrative teams.

- Promotes advancement of the profession through participation in professional organizations.

Continued ▶

The content in this appendix is not current and is of historical significance only.

STANDARDS OF PROFESSIONAL PERFORMANCE

Additional Measurement Criteria for the Advanced Practice Hospice and Palliative Registered Nurse:

The advanced practice hospice and palliative registered nurse:

- Works to influence decision-making bodies to improve patient care.

- Provides direction to enhance the effectiveness of the healthcare team.

- Initiates and revises protocols or guidelines to reflect evidence-based or best practices, to reflect accepted changes in care management, or to address emerging problems.

- Promotes communication of information and advancement of the profession through writing, publishing, and presentations for professional or lay audiences.

- Designs innovations to effect change in practice and improve health outcomes.

Additional Measurement Criteria for the Hospice and Palliative Registered Nurse in a Nursing Role Specialty:

The hospice and palliative registered nurse in a nursing role specialty:

- Works to influence decision-making bodies to improve patient care, health services, and policies.

- Promotes communication of information and advancement of the profession through writing, publishing, and presentations for professional or lay audiences.

- Designs innovations to effect change in practice and outcomes.

- Provides direction to enhance the effectiveness of the multi-disciplinary or interdisciplinary team.

The content in this appendix is not current and is of historical significance only.

GLOSSARY

Admission process. The activity that begins with the initial referral to the program of care and continues through the development of the interdisciplinary plan of care.

Assessment. A systematic, dynamic process in which the nurse, through interaction with the patient and family, significant others, other members of the interdisciplinary healthcare team, and consultants, collects and analyzes data about the patient and family. Data may include physical, psychological, sociocultural, spiritual, cognitive, functional, developmental, economic, and lifestyle dimensions.

Continuity of care. An interdisciplinary process that includes patients and significant others in the development of a coordinated plan of care. This process facilitates the patient's transition between settings, based on changing needs and available resources, across the healthcare continuum.

Criteria. Relevant, measurable indicators of the standards of hospice and palliative nursing practice.

Diagnosis. The analysis and synthesis of the patient history, physical examination, and test results to formulate a hypothesis of an abnormal condition indicated by the anatomy, physiology, or biochemical dysfunction of an organ.

Evaluation. The process of determining both the patient's and the family's progress toward the attainment of expected outcomes and the effectiveness of nursing care, including the patient's value system and goals for care.

Family. People bound by biological or legal ties, or those who define themselves as a "close other" with another person, or "those who function in familistic ways" (Settles, 1987, p. 160). These ways of functioning can include nurturance, intimacy, companionship, and economic, social, psychosocial, spiritual, and physical support in time of need or in illness (adapted from Matocha, 1992).

Healthcare providers. People with special expertise who provide healthcare services or assistance to patients. They must include nurses, physicians, pharmacists, patient care technicians, psychologists, social

The content in this appendix is not current and is of historical significance only.

workers, nutritionists/dietitians, various therapists (such as physical therapists, occupational therapists, and speech and language therapists), and other members of the interdisciplinary team, such as chaplains or spiritual counselors.

Implementation. Any of the following activities: teaching, intervening, delegating, and coordinating. The patient and family or other members of the interdisciplinary healthcare team may be designated to implement interventions in the plan of care.

Interdisciplinary team. A highly qualified, specially trained team of hospice and palliative care professionals and volunteers who work together to meet the physiological, psychological, social, spiritual, and economic needs of the patient and family facing life-limiting, progressive illness and bereavement. The team may include physicians, nurses, social workers, clergy, bereavement counselors, and others as indicated for specific needs.

Life-limiting illness. Any chronic illness that is life threatening and progressively debilitating regardless of age, length of time since diagnosis or functional status.

Nurse. A person licensed by a state agency to practice as a registered nurse.

Nursing. The protection, promotion, and optimization of health and abilities, prevention of illness and injury, alleviation of suffering through the diagnosis and treatment of human response, and advocacy in the care of individuals, families, communities, and populations (ANA, 2003, p. 6).

Nursing diagnosis. A clinical judgment about the patient's and family's response to actual or potential health conditions or needs. Nursing diagnoses most often focus on pain and symptom management and provide the basis for determination of a plan of care to achieve expected outcomes.

Nursing role specialty. An advanced level of nursing practice that intersects with another body of knowledge, has a direct influence on nursing practice, and supports the delivery of direct care rendered to patients by other professional nurses (ANA, 2004, p. 16).

Outcomes. Measurable expected patient- and family-focused goals that translate into observable behaviors.

The content in this appendix is not current and is of historical significance only.

Palliative care continuum. Support and care for people and their families experiencing life-limiting, progressive illness from the time of diagnosis with advanced disease or serious injury through the death of the person and into the bereavement period of the family.

Patient. Recipient of nursing practice. The term *patient* is used in the standards to provide consistency and brevity, bearing in mind that *client* or *individual* might be better choices in some instances. When the patient is one person, the focus is on the health, problems, or needs of that person. When the patient is a family or group, the focus is on the health state of the unit as a whole or the effects of an individual's health on the other members of the unit.

Plan of care. The comprehensive outline of care, written according to the patient's or family's wishes and intended to attain expected outcomes when implemented by the interdisciplinary team.

Resources. Assets that can be drawn upon by the patient and family for aid. Types of resources include, but are not limited to, financial, emotional, spiritual, social, psychological, and physical.

Standard. An authoritative statement enunciated and promulgated by the profession, by which the quality of practice, service, or education can be judged.

Standards of practice. Authoritative statements that describe a competent level of nursing care as demonstrated by the critical thinking model known as the nursing process. The nursing process includes assessment, diagnosis, outcomes identification, planning, implementation, and evaluation. The nursing process encompasses all significant actions taken by registered nurses, and is the foundation of the nurse's decision making (ANA, 2004, p. 4).

Standards of professional performance. Authoritative statements that describe a competent level of behavior in the professional role, including activities related to quality of practice, education, professional practice evaluation, collegiality, collaboration, ethics, research, resource utilization, and leadership (ANA, 2004, p. 4).

Unit of care. The patient with a life-limiting or progressive illness and the patient's family. The patient and family are an interdependent, integrated whole composed of two or more individuals. They experience individual as well as overlapping needs.

The content in this appendix is not current and is of historical significance only.

REFERENCES

American Association of Colleges of Nursing (AACN). (1997). *Peaceful death document.* Washington, DC: AACN.

American Association of Colleges of Nursing (AACN) and City of Hope National Medical Center. (2005). *End-of-Life Nursing Education Consortium (ELNEC) Project.*

American Nurses Association (ANA). (2001). *Code of ethics for nurses with interpretive statements.* Washington, DC: American Nurses Publishing.

American Nurses Association (ANA). (2003). *Pain management and control of distressing symptoms in dying patients.* Available under Position Statements: Ethics and Human Rights at http://www.nursingworld.org.

Center to Advance Palliative Care (CAPC). (2006). *Hospital Palliative Care Programs Continue Rapid Growth.* (December 7, 2006). New York: CAPC. NY. Available at http://www.capc.org/news-and-events/releases/december-2006-release.

Hospice and Palliative Nurses Association (HPNA). (2001). *Professional competencies for generalist hospice and palliative nurses.* Dubuque, IA: Kendall/Hunt.

Hospice and Palliative Nurses Association (HPNA). (2002). *Competencies for advance practice hospice and palliative care nurses.* Dubuque, IA: Kendall/Hunt.

Knaus, W., et al. (1995). A controlled trial to improve care for seriously ill hospitalized patients. *Journal of the American Medical Association 274* (20), 1591–1598.

Last Acts Task Force. (1998). National policy statements on end-of-life care: Precepts of palliative care. *Journal of Palliative Medicine 1,* 109–112.

Matocha, L. K. (1992). Case study interviews: Caring for persons with AIDS. In J. F. Gilgun, K. Daly, & G. Handel (Eds.), *Qualitative methods in family research* (pp. 66–84). Newbury Park, CA: Sage Publications.

The content in this appendix is not current and is of historical significance only.

National Consensus Project for Quality Palliative Care. (2004). *Clinical practice guidelines for quality palliative care.* http://www.nationalconsensusproject.org.

Settles, B. H. (1987). A perspective on tomorrow's families. In M. B. Sussman & S. K. Steinmetz (Eds.), *Handbook of marriage and the family* (pp. 157–180). New York: Plenum.

The content in this appendix is not current and is of historical significance only.

BIBLIOGRAPHY

Billings, J. A., & Block, S. (1997). Palliative care in undergraduate medical education. *Journal of the American Medical Association 278*(9), 733–736.

Dahlin, C. (1999). Access to hospice. In I. Corless & Z. Foster (Eds.), *The hospice heritage: Celebrating the future* (pp. 75–84). New York: The Haworth Press, Inc.

Doyle, D., Hanks, G., & MacDonald, N. (1998). *Oxford textbook of palliative medicine.* New York: Oxford Medical Publication.

Ferris, F., & Cummings, I. (1995). *Palliative care: Towards a consensus in standardized principles of practice.* Ottawa, Ontario: Canadian Palliative Care Association.

Field, M., & Cassel, C. (1997). *Approaching death: Improving care at the end of life.* Washington, DC: National Academies Press.

Portenoy, R., & Bruera, B. (1997). *Topics in palliative care: Volume 1.* New York: Oxford Medical Publications.

Randall, F., & Downie, R. S. (1996). *Palliative care ethics.* New York: Oxford Medical Publications.

Sherman, D. W. (2001). Access to hospice care. *Journal of Palliative Medicine, 3*(4), 407–411.

Index

Note: Entries with [2007] indicate an entry from *Hospice and Palliative Nursing: Scope and Standards of Practice* (2007), reproduced in Appendix A. That information is not current but included for historical value only.